Esther Williamson Ballou

Esther Williamson Ballou. *Photo courtesy of Evelyn Swarthout Hayes.*

Esther Williamson Ballou

A Bio-Bibliography

James R. Heintze

Donald L. Hixon, Series Adviser

Bio-Bibliographies in Music, Number 5

GREENWOOD PRESS
New York • Westport, Connecticut • London

LIBRARY OF CONGRESS CATALOGING-IN-PUBLICATION DATA

Heintze, James R.
   Esther Williamson Ballou: a bio-bibliography.

   (Bio-bibliographies in music, ISSN 0742-6968 ; no. 5)
   Bibliography: p.
   Discography: p.
   Includes index.
   1. Ballou, Esther Williamson, 1915-1973—Bibliography.
2. Ballou, Esther Williamson, 1915-1973—Discography.
3. Music—Bio-bibliography. I. Title. II. Series.
ML134.B16H4 1987   016.78'092'4   86-31797
ISBN 0-313-25069-3 (lib. bdg. : alk. paper)

Library of Congress Catalog Card Number: 86-31797
ISBN: 0-313-25069-3
ISSN: 0742-6968

First published in 1987

Greenwood Press, Inc.
88 Post Road West, Westport, Connecticut 06881

Printed in the United States of America

∞™

The paper used in this book complies with the
Permanent Paper Standard issued by the National
Information Standards Organization (Z39.48-1984).

10 9 8 7 6 5 4 3 2 1

COPYRIGHT ACKNOWLEDGMENTS

Materials from Esther Ballou's Personal Papers are cited
in this book with permission from the American University Archives.

Contents

Preface

The first time I met Esther Ballou was during the late sixties at The American University in Washington, D.C. where I was pursuing a graduate degree in music. Esther was teaching a course on orchestration and I had the good fortune to have been one of her students. I truly enjoyed her classes, which she seemed to have conducted without the benefit of prepared notes. Without lecturing, she led us to discover our musical abilities and how we could express them to others. I was most impressed with her versatility as a musician; she was equally skilled as a composer, pianist, and teacher. She was certainly the best sight reader I had ever heard. On one occasion, literally minutes before a student was to perform in a recital, the accompanist was no where to be found, and Esther was asked if she would accompany the student in a work by Brahms. I remember hurrying to the recital hall, not to hear the student, but rather Esther's performance. When it was over, I wondered how it was possible that anyone could have performed that work with such polish and technical accuracy without any preparation.

I admired Esther greatly as a musician and person, and was stunned when told that she would not be returning from her trip to England. A few days after her death, on the evening of March 28, 1973, a quiet, yet lovely, concert and eulogy were presented in memory of her at American University. It was then that her composer's creed, a candid and moving statement of self-evaluation written in September 1970, had its first public reading by Lloyd Ultan. It seems fitting to include that statement in this volume.

During the years that followed, I met many times with her husband Harold in their home to discuss the progress made in the establishment of a memorial collection of Esther's manuscripts and personal papers at American University, and the preparation of a brief biographical article, later published in the New Grove Dictionary of Music and Musicians (see: B91). Those visits helped me obtain a personal insight into Esther's life and provided the inspiration for the present work. Although her music has continued to be performed

over the years since her death, it seems especially appropri-
ate that now, for the first time, a study of her life and
contributions to the musical world, is available in print.
     This volume consists of four principal sections, includ-
ing: (1) a biography; (2) a complete list of works and performances arranged by subject and then cited alphabetically
by title of composition. Following each title is, if known,
the premiere of the work and other selected performances,
including references to commentaries from reviews of performances cited in the "Bibliography." Each work is assigned an
entry number preceded by the designation "W" for Work (W1,
W2, W3, etc.). Each performance of that work is assigned a
successive lower-case letter (W1a, W1b, W1c, etc.); (3) an
annotated bibliography of writings by and about Esther
Ballou. For reviews of her music cited in this section, I
have quoted only those portions of the reviews which refer
directly to her music. Each entry is assigned an entry
number preceded by the designation "B" for "Bibliography"
(B1, B2, B3, etc.). I have identified those writings that
contain photographs of the composer. See references refer to
the "Works and Performances" and "Discography" appendix.
     Included also are five appendixes: (1) a discography;
(2) interviews and other audio sources on Ballou, including
her participation in a television panel discusion, and her
appearance on a televised children's show; (3) a self-
evaluation by the composer; (4) a list of her compositions
arranged alphabetically; and (5) a list of her compositions
arranged chronologically. Following is a complete index of
names (personal and corporate) and titles.
     Much of the research is based upon the composer's per-
sonal papers held in the American University Archives. Those
papers include her manuscripts, drafts of her writings, correspondence, reviews of performances, photographs, business
records, class notes, student papers, marginal notes, recordings, and other documents. However, some of the information
contained therein had to be confirmed using other sources
because of omitted detail such as accurate dates, complete
names of individuals, page numbers, etc. In an effort to be
accurate and to obtain information not contained in those
papers, I conducted an extensive bibliographical search on
the composer, and contacted many of her friends and colleagues.

MANUSCRIPT COLLECTIONS

     Most of Esther Ballou's manuscripts and sketches are
held in the American University Archives in Washington, D.C.
Some of the manuscripts have been revised; others contain
slight editorial changes which were made by Esther when she
heard her works for the first time in rehearsal. The edi-

torial markings and revisions are not necessarily noted,
however, on the photocopied manuscripts currently available
from American Composers Alliance in New York. I have noted
revisions where they apply for certain compositions in the
"Works and Performances" section. I have not been able to
locate copies of the following manuscripts: <u>Triumphant Figure</u>
for piano (W78), <u>Earth Saga</u> for piano (four hands) (W104),
<u>Fugato</u> for five winds and three brass instruments (W105),
<u>Lysistrata</u> (W106), <u>Madchen in Uniform</u> (W107), and <u>Tree of
Sins</u> for soprano, piano, and percussion (W114).
     For information on obtaining photocopies of Ballou's
scores held in the American University Archives, contact the
University Archivist, American University Library, 4400
Massachusetts Avenue, Washington, D.C., 20016. Copies of
many of Ballou's works are available from American Composers
Alliance, whose address is 170 West 74th Street, New York,
N.Y., 10023. In addition, the Sibley Music Library of the
Eastman School of Music has copies of W10, W12, W13, W24,
W25, W32, W34, W38, W39, W53, W56, W62, and W72; the
Dickinson Music Library of Vassar College has copies of W13,
W24, W25, W39, W41, and W80; the library at Bennington
College has copies of W1, W41, and W56; and the Edwin A.
Fleisher Collection of Orchestral Music in the Free Library
of Philadelphia has copies of W5, W12, and W13. (<u>See</u>: B69.)
Other institutions whose libraries hold one or more copies of
her scores include: California State University at Hayward,
Florida State University, Oberlin Conservatory of Music, San
Francisco State University, University of Arizona, University
of California at Irvine, University of New Mexico, and
Wheaton College.

Acknowledgments

The research for this volume was made possible by a
sabbatical leave award for 1985 and 1986 from American
University. Initial thanks must be extended to Donald D.
Dennis, University Librarian, American University, who
supported this leave.
Many persons and institutions contributed to the preparation of this volume. In particular, I should like to
offer special thanks to the following individuals.

For providing specialized bio-bibliographical assistance
(in alphabetical order):

Harold Ballou; Tommie E. Carl, President and Founder,
American Women Composers, Inc.; Charles Crowder, Director of
Music, Phillips Gallery, and Department of Performing Arts,
American University; Julian DeGray, pianist; Selma Epstein,
pianist; Lou Harrison, composer; Evelyn Swarthout Hayes,
pianist, DPA, American University; Winifred Hyson, composer;
Ellis B. Kohs, composer; Otto Luening, composer; Robert G.
McBride, composer; Alan Mandel, pianist, DPA, American Uni-
versity; Vito Mason, conductor, DPA, American University;
Mary Natvig, Reference Assistant, Sibley Music Library of the
Eastman School of Music; Leanne Rees, pianist; Jerzy
Sapieyevski, composer, DPA, American University; Charlotte
Shear, Historian, Friday Morning Music Club; Gordon H. Smith,
composer, DPA, American University; Rebecca B. Stickney,
Special Assistant to the President, Bennington College; Lloyd
Ultan, Chairman, School of Music, University of Minnesota;
Sabrina L. Weiss, Music Librarian, Vassar College.

For providing assistance in the organization of Ballou's
personal papers (in alphabetical order):

William A. Banks, Assistant Music Librarian, American University Library; Thomas A. Devan, Assistant Archivist, American University; Kathy Foley, Student Assistant, American University Library; Martha Mac Intire, Student Assistant, American University Library; William Ross, Archivist, American University.

For providing editorial assistance:

Donald L. Hixon, Fine Arts Librarian at the University of California at Irvine and Adviser for the series Bio-Bibliographies in Music.

Finally, I must thank my wife, Yolanda Aguirre, who encouraged me to pursue this project, and most important, my parents, Ruth and Gustav, who provided my early musical training.

Esther Williamson Ballou

Biography

Esther Louise Williamson Ballou was born in Elmira, New York, July 17, 1915, the daughter of Mr. and Mrs. E. Duff and Marbury (Clark) Williamson. She spent her childhood at 103 Lexington Avenue[1] and began piano lessons at the age of four with Evelyn Bosworth.

> I realize now how fortunate I was in the beginning. The feeling for music was not only encouraged in the home, but my teacher too communicated a respect and love for its beauty.[2]

Both of her parents enjoyed singing and, at the age of five, the little musician was already accompanying her father on piano. In her words:

> He had a rich, natural baritone voice, with little formal training in music. He would make me play the way he wanted the song to be sung. This caused me great difficulty with some of my music teachers; I wouldn't follow the proper rhythm.[3]

She attended Grace Episcopal Church and the musical services likely helped influence her decision to begin organ lessons at the age of thirteen.[4] The lessons continued for six years. During this time, her keyboard facility had developed so well that she often performed piano over Elmira radio station WESG. She not only played solo jazz and classical music, but also "accompanied many singers and instrumentalists in their broadcasts."[5] During the winter of 1932, Ballou prepared for an organ recital which took place at her church on March 20, 1932. She performed works by Bach, Wagner, and Franck.[6] On February 14, 1933, she performed the Schumann Piano Concerto with the Elmira Symphony Orchestra in Elmira.[7]

In the fall of 1933 she entered Bennington College with a scholarship in music. Her studies included piano with Julian DeGray and composition with Otto Luening. A close friendship was developed by Ballou with DeGray, and was to

last throughout her lifetime.[8] Luening, who thought Ballou
was "naturally very talented," introduced her to various
forms of instrumental writing which included her first
contrapuntal studies.[9]

From 1933-1938, Ballou served as accompanist for the
Bennington Summer School for the Dance, an important forum
for modern dance at that time. Summer sessions lasted for
six weeks.[10] It was here that she first expressed an
interest in composition. She composed piano accompaniments
for modern dance techniques used by Martha Hill, Bessie
Schoenberg, and Doris Humphrey.[11] "I was. . . accompanying
for them and improvising. . . and this led immediately into
composition, and thats how it all began."[12] Each accompaniment was used for a specific movement and provided a means
for an extended improvisation by the accompanist. These
accompaniments, carefully noted by Ballou, are unique and
historically valuable.[13] By examining the actual music used
in these classes, one has a better musical understanding of
what Hill, Schoenberg, and Humphrey were trying to accom-
plish. By having composed these accompaniments, Ballou
provided a musical impetus to the modern dance movement, and
deserves, therefore, to be remembered for her part in the
development of that movement. The experience she acquired
from working with these pioneers in the modern dance movement
was also vital to her musical development, and led to collab-
orations with other dancers. "All these people were coming
into their own at that time, and it was a very exciting time
to be there."[14]

During the winter of 1936, she began work on a piano and
clarinet duet titled Impertinence, which was completed on
April 6. On November 7 of that year, Robert McBride, who was
a member of the faculty at Bennington, and Ballou travelled
to New York to perform the work over radio station WABC.[15] A
feature article on Ballou in a local newspaper announced the
forthcoming broadcast and stated further that "The rise of
the young Elmiran in the musical world has been steady and
brilliant. Recently Miss Williamson composed a group of
modern dance numbers, and gave them in a recital at Bennington. She is said to be especially adept at this type of
work, which is highly difficult."[16] In order to earn expense
money at Bennington, she also taught piano privately after
classes. Each year she spent the winter break in New York,
usually staying with families of fellow students. Expense
money was earned by accompanying dance classes at New York
University.[17] She graduated from Bennington in June 1937.

In September 1937, she received a fellowship in composition from Mills College and moved to California. She studied
composition there with Domenico Brescia, "a very charming,
wonderful teacher."[18] She later commented on her experience
in California:

While at Mills, I played several solo concerts as well as two pianos with Elizabeth Wilton, one of these being the Bach Two Piano Concerto with the Berkeley Symphony under Albert Elkus. I wrote the music for the Mills College production of "Madchen in Uniform" and conducted the premiere performance in the Geary Theater in San Francisco. Also wrote many compositions for dance during this time.[19]

Ballou spent a great deal of time as a dance accompanist there, and continued to work with the Bennington School of Dance when they held classes on the Mills campus during the summer of 1938. At that time she also worked with dancers Hanya Holm and Marian Van Tuyl. "While still a student at Mills College, Miss Williamson completed the ballets Earth Saga for Louise Kloepper and Lysistrata for José Limón. . . ."[20] She graduated from Mills College in the spring of 1938. Her master's thesis project was a Violin and Pianoforte Sonata. In 1939, she toured with dancers Irene Alonso and Leola Harlow for a number of Spanish dance concerts on the East coast. On these programs, when the dancers changed costumes and rested, Ballou would perform a group of solo pieces, usually by Spanish composers.[21] In March 1940, Ballou was back at Mills College completing a score and screen play for an educational animated film starring Mickey and Minnie Mouse. This delightful frolic has three scenes: "Class in Music," "Practice Scenes," and "Fugue." The opening scene finds Mickey and Minnie and other students in "Music School." The professor is teaching the art of fugal writing and assigns the characters the task of composing a subject, "with no less than three countersubjects." The rest of the film depicts our little friends at meeting their assigned task.[22] It was at this time that Ballou was offered a position working at the Walt Disney studios. She declined the offer.[23]

Most of the pieces that Ballou composed during the late thirties and early forties are in smaller forms and include Jazz Theme and Variations for Piano (1936), Dance Suite (1937) for piano, Country Dance for Piano (1937), In Blues Tempo (1937) for clarinet and piano, Nocturne for String Quartet (1937), Preludes for Piano (1940-1941), and a number of songs from 1937-1938. Characteristically, these works are tonal, yet mildly dissonant, and rhythmically alive. Some of these compositions were among her first attempts at incorporating jazz elements into her writing. Some years later she reflected, "I have always liked jazz, of course--the rhythm and the vitality of it, the American quality, the bounce, the effervescence, the spontaneity, I think is the best quality about jazz."[24] During the summer of 1940, Ballou completed the background music for a ballet titled War Lyrics, the music for four-hand piano and trumpet. The choreography was

by José Limón. Not long after, she also collaborated with
Limón on a two-page ballet titled Pop Goes the Weasel (1943).
    In 1940, Ballou moved to New York and found an apartment
at 67 Riverside Drive. She began working on a degree in composition at the Juilliard School of Music, studying composition there with Bernard Wagonaar. She also studied privately
with Wallingford Riegger. When she was not devoting time to
composing, she was busy practicing for recitals. For example, on November 13, 1942, she accompanied the celebrated
dancer Angna Enters at the Sterling Opera House in Derby,
Connecticut. Performed was the well-known "Theatre of Angna
Enters" program in which Enters presented her popular
"Feline" to the music of Debussy, and "Pique-Nique" to the
music of Delibes.[25]
    In 1943, Ballou completed Intermezzo, her first work for
orchestra. In June of that year, she graduated from
Juilliard.

> After that, I taught at the Juilliard School, first
> in the Institute of Musical Art, and then when Mr.
> [William] Schuman came, I was kept on the faculty and
> I taught in the literature and materials department
> there. That was the beginning of the new Juilliard
> which was very exciting, terribly exciting to be a
> part of it.[26]

The courses Ballou taught included theory, harmony, beginning
composition, and ear training. It was in these classes that
she began to experiment with her own innovative ideas in
teaching.[27] Those ideas likely included teaching on a one-
to-one basis, without the use of prepared lectures. In
addition, a creative approach to teaching which was used at
Bennington might have influenced her method of teaching. She
stayed at Juilliard until June 1950.
    On April 1, 1945, Ballou became a member of American
Composers Alliance which gave her the opportunity to distrib-
ute her music to a much wider audience. She was on the road
to greater fortune when, in 1945, while working on her first
piano concerto, she was struck with a severe arthritic illness. "'This took 10 years out of my life. . . . I spent
several years in bed and then in a wheel chair and hobbling
around on crutches.'"[28] She was left with a permanent disa-
bility, evident throughout the lower part of her body. She
would never be able to sit upright at the piano, and a career
as an organist was no longer possible. She endured such
physical stress that she discontinued work on her piano concerto; she had completed only sketches of the first movement.
Not until 1948 did she take up pen to begin composing again.
At that time she began experimenting with the use of twelve-
tone rows. In June 1948, she completed a three-page Prelude
and Gigue for Piano, based on a tone row. Another short
work, titled simply, "A Song," to words by Ben Hamilton, was
completed in January 1949. Her inspiration and motivation

finally returned with the completion of a larger work in
1949, a <u>Sonata for Two Pianos</u>. It proved to be one of her
best compositions and was the first to be commercially published. With a renewed sense of determination, she devoted
more of her time to the arts. In a quest to learn, she read
numerous works of literary merit, all the while making notes
of each item. In February 1949, she wrote two short stories.
She commented later about this period of her life:

> This took 10 years out of my life. That's why I'm
> writing so frantically; I feel so far behind. . . .
> But that's all behind me. It's like talking about
> another person now. I have forgotten just what it
> was like. One does forget these things, thank
> heaven.[29]

In August 1949, she was in Middlebury, Vermont as a
member of a Composers' Conference which "provided experienced
criticism of scores and a program of discussion, instruction,
and performance. . . for those interested in composing
professionally." In addition to Ballou, the teaching staff
included Ingolf Dahl, Richard Dana, Carter Harman, and Otto
Luening.[30] In subsequent years, the Composers' Conference
was held at Bennington College. Ballou participated in the
Conference until 1954.

In 1950, she completed her <u>Forty Finger Beguine</u> for four
pianists on two pianos. This composition was vibrant and reflected a new sense of direction. The composer described it
as "'very jazzy, very gay.'" The work had special meaning
for her; in 1957, she arranged it for two pianists on two
pianos, and in 1962 for full orchestra. Regarding the
<u>Beguine</u>'s first performance for a recital by four piano stu-
dents, Ballou commented that "'they had two pianos lined up
and four girls sitting down, looking just like little birds
and counting like mad. But they played it very well.'"[31]

During this period, Ballou began working with lyricist
Jerry Rand on a musical comedy called <u>Pocohantas Goes to
London</u>. Only the lyrics, a prologue, "Pocohantas Saved John
Smith," a chorus, "Virginia Laid Her Claim for Fame," and two
songs, "Home is a Feeling" and "Just as You Are," were com-
pleted.

In 1950, at the age of thirty-five, Esther fell in love
with Harold Ballou, who, although not a musician, was a fer-
vent supporter of her work.

> He's not a musician, but he's very intelligent and a
> very astute critic; in fact, he's my best critic.
> When I write something, I play it for him first,
> because its very important to get the reaction of a
> person who is not a schooled musician.[32]

They were married in Washington, D.C. on August 10, 1950,[33] and decided to establish permanent residence there. They found a pleasant one-level home surrounded by trees located at 8909 Connecticut Avenue in Chevy Chase, Maryland, a short distance from in-town activities.
Washington was musically an ideal setting for Ballou.

> I love Washington. Its a wonderful place to work and
> to be a musician; especially to be a composer in
> Washington is a very exciting thing, because you can
> get all the performances you could possibly want.
> You can get things played immediately.[34]

She also had numerous opportunites to perform in Washington. For example, on December 30, 1950, in one of her first Washington recitals, she gave the first performance there of Ellis B. Kohs' Piano Variations and Toccata at the Music Teachers National Association annual meeting. She also performed frequently at the Phillips Gallery, both as a soloist and together with other musicians. At times, she presented her own works. In almost all cases, her own performances and compositions were warmly received by both critics and audiences. For example, on December 21, 1953, she and pianist Harry McClure played her Sonata for Two Pianos.[35] And on March 7, 1955, she gave the first performance of her Sonata for Piano. About the latter work one critic noted, "Her music, unlike some contemporary writing for piano, remembers the singing qualities of the instrument as well as some of its finest sonorities."[36] The work was composed in memory of Ruth Crawford Seeger, a close friend of Ballou. The three movements serve as a "protest" about Seeger's death, "meditation," and a "prayer."[37] After a performance of the same work a few months later, another critic noted:

> The bare and angular proclamations of the first
> section are as mystifying as are the deviously
> twisting lines of a following andante. But the
> elusiveness is arresting, for the voice is confident,
> the technique and invention perfectly assured. The
> final Chorale Variations have the same authority,
> with a logic that is much more intelligible on first
> hearing.[38]

On March 19, 1956, she premiered her Trio for Violin, Violoncello, and Piano with the assistance of James Barber, violinist, and John Engberg, cellist. A critic commented, "This is a work that ought to be taken up by any piano trio in search of something new that will at once make its way with audiences. There is an unusual factor in this composer who has a fine gift for writing well and at the same time in a way that attracts musicians and amateurs."[39] Another critic wrote regarding the Sonata and Trio after a performance

in New York, "Both used a modified twelve-tone technique in
their slow movements, but without destroying a strong basic
impression of tonality."[40] As a pianist, the following
comments were typical of those who heard her perform: ". . .
a gifted and sensitive pianist, . . . Esther Ballou played
all these piano parts deftly, musically and with an exquisite
sense of ensemble."[41] During this period, Ballou performed
at a number of other places, including Constitution Hall and,
as a performing member of the Friday Morning Music Club, at
the Cosmos Club Assembly Hall.

Being in Washington also caused Ballou's reputation as a
composer to increase significantly. Practically all of her
compositions from the fifties and sixties were commissioned
works for a variety of ensembles. Some of her best works
during the early and mid-fifties include: <u>Prelude and Allegro
for String Orchestra and Piano</u> (1951), which resulted in her
first commercial recording, <u>Music for the Theatre</u> (1952) for
two pianos, <u>Oboe Concertino for String Orchestra and Oboe</u>
(1953), and <u>Suite for Winds</u> (1957).

From 1951 to 1954, Ballou taught piano and theory in the
Preparatory Department at Catholic University. And for many
years, she also taught privately in her home. During the
summer of 1954, she was a resident fellow at the MacDowell
Colony at Peterborough, New Hampshire.

In 1955, Ballou began teaching at American University.
Her classes included theory, harmony, counterpoint, orchestration, ear training and sight singing, and music appreciation at the college level, and theory and music appreciation
at the pre-college level in the Preparatory Program. She was
instrumental in developing an innovative theory program at
American University and one that served as a model for similar programs at other colleges. The program consisted of six
semesters and was experimental in that it covered in chrono-
logical order the most important developments of "musical
styles, techniques, and practices" in classical music. The
program was devised by members of the teaching faculty, including Ballou, Lloyd Ultan, and James McLain with assistance
from other members of the faculty. In Ballou's words, "equal
emphasis" was placed on "ear training (dictation and sight-
singing) based on the students' own work as well as on the
literature being studied at the time; analysis of the literature; and creative writing based on the literature being
studied. . . . One important premise remains foremost
throughout the program. Factual knowledge is *not* the
starting point, but rather, the result of exploration of the
potentials of the area being investigated." Ballou taught
the first and last semesters in the program. "The first seg-
ment of the program is devoted to rhythm, dynamics, canonic
writing, simple formal relationships, and rhythm-related
vocabulary." She used a number of imaginative procedures for
teaching these elements, including one which was a carryover
from her time at Bennington:

Students from the Modern Dance Department of A.U.
often prepare a dance that is performed for the music
class several times without any accompaniment other
than oral counting. Each music student chooses one
of the dances and composes an accompaniment for it,
to be performed with the dance.[42]

During the late fifties, Ballou composed several works,
including Sonata for Two Pianos No. 2 (1958), Divertimento
for String Quartet (1958), Variations, Scherzo and Fugue on a
Theme by Lou Harrison (1959) for piano, A Babe is Born (1959)
for chorus, and What if a Much of a Which of a Wind (1959)
for three voices and instrumental ensemble.

During the sixties, Ballou gave a number of recitals at
American University, the Phillips Gallery, Corcoran Gallery,
Barker Hall of the Y.W.C.A., National Institutes of Health,
and the French and Mexican embassies. She enjoyed especially
performing four-hand and two-piano works, and played
frequently with her American University colleagues Evelyn
Swarthout and Charles Crowder. She appeared often as a lec-
turer and panelist, and was also interviewed on radio and
television several times. Some of her papers and presentations included: "Sounds that Make Music," American University, November 3, 1962; "Ensemble Playing: Piano Duets," with
Evelyn Swarthout, American University, February 9, 1963; "The
Composer and His Audience," National Symphony Orchestra
Women's Committee meeting, April 10, 1963; and "Interpretation of Keyboard Music During the Romantic Period," Maryland
State Music Teachers Association Workshop, Peabody Conservatory of Music, June 25, 1963. She was also a member of
numerous professional organizations, and was asked to adjudi-
cate for a number of competitions, including, for example in
1971, the National Federation of Music Clubs National Composition Contest for Young Composers, and the National Screen-
ing Committee for the Fulbright-Hays Grants in Composition.

From 1960-1969, Ballou composed at least 35 compositions
for a variety of ensembles. Some of the more significant
compositions from the early sixties include: Beguine (1960),
arranged for orchestra and premiered by the National Symphony
Orchestra; In Memoriam for Oboe and String Orchestra (1960),
originally the second movement of the Oboe Concertino for
String Orchestra and Oboe and composed in memory of Walter
Penland, an oboist who premiered the original work but later
died in an airplane crash; Street Scenes (1960), a group of
four songs for voice and piano; Brass Sextette with Pianoforte (1962); Early American Portrait (1962) for soprano and
orchestra; and "The Sea in Maine: The Presence of the Sea"
(August 1962), a song for baritone and piano composed in
Stonington, Maine.

Street Scenes, based on the seasons, represents Ballou's
second cycle consisting of four songs; the first was composed
in 1937. She described the work on television, prior to a
live performance, in this way:

Each of these seasons of the year has a special
character. The summer is very soft and gentle as you
will hear and there are very soft chords and thirds
and [a] smooth melodic line. The next song is about
autumn, the crisp time of the year when you have this
kind of second [interval]; you see this makes it sort
of pert and exciting. And then you have the dotted
rhythm, and its about a maple tree which is tossing
her leaves to the throng. The next one is about
winter. This is a cold, cold time of the year. You
will hear the major seventh interval. And you will
hear all kinds of minor seconds here to bring out the
cold. And then there's someting about Jack Frost a
little later on too, talking about the carpet of ice
and snow he spreads, and you can hear that up in this
part of the piano. And the last one is about spring,
that elusive lady who comes and goes. Sometimes
she's very sweet and pleasant and sometimes it pours
rain. And she's going to rain in the middle here in
the song.[43]

The more significant composition composed during this period
was Capriccio for Violin and Piano (1963); it was the first
work by a woman composer to be premiered at the White House.
The composition was commissioned for the Young Artist Compe-
tition Winners Concert by the District of Columbia Federation
of Music Clubs and was performed in the East Room on September 6, 1963. It is a difficult piece, rather serious, and
not really a capriccio in the usual sense. One critic noted
about the premiere:

It is an intense piece that is filled with strong
musical ideas. . . . It is an angry piece that cuts
a sharp swath toward being downright furious but
relinquishes its culmination in favor of more savory
cadences. . . . It is a jewel from the pen of Mrs.
Ballou and is certainly a valuable addition to the
violin repertory.[44]

Ivan Romenenko, a violinist who performed the work at the
Phillips Gallery in Washington, D.C. in December 1966, was
impressed with it:

It is quite an unusual piece. I never faced before,
in my entire musical life, [a] composition which has
more musical demands than technical [demands]. . . .
Technically, its extremely difficult in some parts. .
. . Its a quiet piece with unusual sonorities.[45]

On June 7, 1964, Ballou was awarded an honorary Doctor
of Humane Letters from Hood College. She was cited for her
"effective dedication to her dream of creating beauty and for
the many hours of musical delight she has given her listeners

in this country and abroad," and was considered "a remarkable
musician, composer, and educator."[46]
    During the mid to late sixties, Ballou composed a number
of significant compositions, including: Concerto for Piano
and Orchestra (1964); Concerto for Solo Guitar and Chamber
Orchestra (1964); three choral works, including I Will Lift
Up Mine Eyes (1965), May the Words (1965), and Hear Us!
(1967); 5-4-3 (1966) for mezzo-contralto, viola, and harp;
Impromptu for Organ (1968); Konzertstück for Viola and Orchestra (1969); and Prism for String Trio (1969).
    The Concerto for Piano, for example, was commissioned by
the National Gallery Orchestra for their 1000th concert at
the National Gallery of Art, and was written specifically for
Charles Crowder, pianist, who premiered it on June 6, 1965.
"Cast in more than three movements, like concertos of those
other 'B' composers Brahms and Busoni, the new work is in the
big, romantic manner."[46] In the fourth movement, Ballou used
a cryptic device for determining what the theme would be.
She explained:

> Main theme in IV movement derived from the name of
> the pianist for whom the Concerto was written,
> Charles Crowder. However I used "Chuck" Crowder
> (altho' it doesn't fit his elegance)--but "Charles"
> didn't make a good theme for my purposes.[47]

Starting with middle C which is assigned the letter "a," each
pitch in the chromatic scale is assigned a subsequent letter
of the alphabet, "a" through "z." For example, B-flat above
middle C is assigned the letter "k." The theme is first used
in its entirety by the bassoons in measures 10-11.
    Another important work during this period, and one which
was commissioned by the Kindler Foundation, was 5-4-3 ("five"
songs "for" "three" performers). Ballou described the songs
during an interview:

> They are of all various kinds of mood. The first one
> I had such fun doing, because the harp can be muted
> which I hadn't experienced before. What the harpist
> does is to take a piece of a super market shopping
> bag, you know, this heavy paper, and make a long
> strip and weave it within the strings. . . . It
> rattles. . ., and this makes the kind of chatter
> which I wanted. . . . And then I used another de-
> vice, which is most interesting in the harp. In the
> last song ["!hope"] its about bells ringing and I use
> this glissando effect, you know, in the bass strings
> of the harp with moving the pedal quickly so that you
> get a drone sort of effect, like a bell. [The second
> song] is about the moon and is quite impresssionistic
> and lots of glissandos, soft glissandos in the harp.
> The next one is "May i be gay," which is about a lark

singing, and I took the songs of the birds in my own
backyard in Maryland.[48]

During 1970-1971, much of Ballou's time was spent working on her new textbook "Creative Explorations of Musical
Elements." This work was to serve as a teacher's manual for
beginning theory courses. It represents, perhaps, best of
all her own methodology used in introducing students to basic
elements in music. By September 1971, she had completed the
work, and forwarded a copy to her publisher (Holt, Rinehart,
and Winston) for editorial approval.[49]

In June 1971, Ballou performed at the White House for
First Lady Patricia Nixon when the latter was initiated an
honorary patroness of Sigma Alpha Iota.[50] In February 1972,
she was commissioned by Charles Crowder, Music Director of
the Phillips Gallery, to compose a work in honor of Elmira
Bier on the occasion of her retirement from the gallery.[51]
The work Ballou chose was a string quartet and was to be her
last completed work. By spring 1972, she had finished
writing the quartet titled Un Morceau d'Ensemble sur le nom
d'Elmira. It was premiered on June 10 of that year, and was
considered by one critic to be "an inventive piece."[52]

In July 1972, Ballou made plans to travel to England on
her 1972-1973 sabbatical leave from American University. Her
goals were to devote much of her time to composing and to
complete a number of commissioned works. In addition, she
planned, in her own words: "to investigate the new educational experiments which originated in Leicester, England, under
the direction of Mr. Roy Illsley and known as the 'open
classroom' theory of education. . . . The 'open classroom'
technique has an underlying philosophy that parallels my own,
as exemplified both in my own classroom teaching and in the
premises stated in my recently completed book."[53]

During the summer of 1972, however, she was stricken
with an illness which demanded immediate hospitalization and
surgery. She seemed to have recovered and so commenced plans
for travelling by boat to England. By September she was in
England residing in Magnolia Cottage in Felpham. In November
she received a commission by the British National Youth
Orchestra to compose a piano concerto, and to perform as
soloist in its premiere on the Isle of Man in April of the
following year.[54] On November 26, she attended a concert by
the Kathleen Merritt Orchestra at Steep Church in
Petersfield; it was likely the last performance she heard.
In early December, she was ill again. Her condition grew
steadily worse. Surgery was performed on January 12 at St.
Richard's Hospital in Chichester. Her condition, however,
continued to deteriorate. She died on March 12 in
Chichester.

Esther Ballou composed over one hundred works, a testa-
ment to an outstanding musical career. Most of her music was
commissioned which accounts for the larger number of works

written for small ensembles, voice, and piano. Her style of
composition covered a broad spectrum of ideas and treatment,
including jazz, folk idioms, dance, twelve-tone music, and an
occasional experiment with special effects. On the whole,
she followed a more conservative approach, often relying upon
a strong melodic line and focusing on basic chordal elements,
such as fourths and fifths used alone or in clusters, in
order to achieve linear cohesion and structural balance. She
described her music in this way:

> [My music] tends towards classicism in that it
> stresses clarity of design and directness of expres-
> sion. I am very conscious of lucidity and unity of
> texture and I try to achieve balance and direction.
> Rhythm and all its connotations are of especial in-
> terest to me and the music of Wallingford Riegger and
> Elliott Carter seem to me to be the most representa-
> tive of what I like best in contemporary music.[55]

Of the source of her musical ideas, she explained:

> Sometimes you read a poem which inspires you. Some-
> times, you have an experience which somehow you'd
> like to translate into sound. Every composer is very
> different, though. You may get a very good idea and
> not use it for years and years. And then, suddenly,
> you decide to work on this, to work it out. . . . I
> think inspiration can give you a very minute idea,
> but the craft of working it out is anything but in-
> spirational. It's just plain hard work.[56]

Ballou was loved and admired by those who knew her. Her
special abilities as not only a composer, but also as a
pianist and educator inspired others. Robert Parris once
commented on her influence in Washington, D.C.:

> The appearance of Esther Williamson Ballou in Wash-
> ington was a happy occurrence all the way around.
> She stimulated many people, not only as a composer
> but also as [a] performer and teacher, and an in-
> crease in this city's professional standards has
> without doubt resulted from her presence on the
> musical scene here.[57]

Perhaps the most fitting tribute has come from Lloyd Ultan,
composer, educator, and friend:

> Dr. Ballou is probably the most genuinely loved
> teacher I have ever had the pleasure of knowing. She
> is admired (almost revered) by her students and is
> dedicated to making them achieve the highest
> standards possible. She is a demanding teacher who
> works with imagination and a creative spirit and

talent unique in the profession. Professionally, Dr.
Ballou has achieved some of the finest recognition
open to her. She is one of the few women composers
recognized, performed and recorded, and is not
considered only in the light of being a woman composer but a composer, by any criteria, of the highest
caliber. . . . Dr. Ballou deserves the highest re-
spect as both a teacher and an artist. She is, in
addition, one of the finest human beings a person
could hope to know. A brilliant, yet humble, person
who is loved by her students and colleagues alike.[58]

1. "Ballou, Esther Williamson." Who's Who in the East. 14th
    ed. (Chicago: Marquis, 1973), p. 33. Her date of birth
    appears in several places among her personal papers.
    Statements which are not footnoted are based on
    Ballou's personal papers held in the American Universi-
    ty Archives.
2. Faith Frome, "Spotlight--A Composer: She's Teaching Kids
    How to Hear Music," Montgomery County Sentinel (16 July
    1964), p. B7.
3. Eric Shaffer, Biography of Esther Ballou, untitled
    typescript, American University Archives (December 14,
    1971), p. 1.
4. Although not known for sure, she might have studied organ
    with William H. Morvan, "organist and Master of the
    Choristers." Grace Church, Elmira, N.Y. "The Weekly
    Message" (20 March 1932) in American University
    Archives.
5. "Elmira Girl. . . " Elmira Advertiser (6 November 1936).
6. "Weekly Message" (20 March 1932).
7. Program notes, Elmira Symphony Orchestra (February 14,
    1933) in American University Archives.
8. Many years later, whenever Ballou visited DeGray, she
    would request a piano lesson. See, for example, letter
    from EWB to Julian DeGray, 9 November 1971 (C60).
9. Otto Luening, telephone conversation with the author, 18
    March 1986.
10. John Martin, America Dancing (New York: Dodge, 1936), p.
    177.
11. Humphrey's technique classes met every day in the morning
    for two hours. Each afternoon she conducted a two-hour
    class in composition, and rehearsals were in the
    evening. Selma Jeanne Cohen, Doris Humphrey: An Artist
    First (Middletown, Conn.: (Wesleyan University, 1972),
    p. 140. Otto Luening also provides an account of the
    Bennington dance activities in his Odyssey of an Ameri-
    can Composer: The Autobiography of Otto Luening (New
    York: Charles Scribner's Sons, 1980), pp. 398-99.

12. Gordon Smith, interview with Esther Ballou, Washington,
    D.C., 28 March 1962.
13. Some of these accompaniments are in the American Univer-
    sity Achives. <u>See</u>: W102
14. Smith, interview, 28 March 1962.
15. McBride recalls that the piece "was a short, fast,
    razzle-dazzle pop-type in which she tickled the ivorys
    like Zez Confrey." Robert McBride, letter to the
    author, 11 March 1986.
16. "Elmira Girl. . ." (November 6, 1936). Some of Ballou's
    dances composed at Bennington in 1937 included a
    "Rigaudon," "Galliarde," "Courante," "Bouree," and
    "Gigue." <u>See</u>: W53
17. Thomas P. Brockway, <u>Bennington College: In the Beginning</u>
    (Bennington: Bennington College Press, 1981), pp. 161-
    62.
18. Smith, interview, 28 March 1962.
19. Esther Ballou personal papers, American University
    Archives. <u>Madchen in Uniform</u> is unlocated. However,
    Ballou wrote a <u>Suite for Chamber Orchestra</u> (April 1939)
    which was, as she noted, "derived" from <u>Madchen</u>. The
    <u>Suite</u> has similar melodic elements as a later produc-
    tion titled <u>War Lyrics</u> (July 1940). The connection be-
    tween these three compositions is unclear. <u>See</u>: W107,
    W14, W116, respectively
20. Richard Donald Ringenwald, "The Music of Esther
    Williamson Ballou: An Analytical Study" (M.A. thesis,
    American University, 1960), p. 2. Kloepper was a
    Bennington Fellow in the Summer of 1938. Barbara N.
    Cohen-Stratyner, "Louise Kloepper," <u>Biographical</u>
    <u>Dictionary of Dance</u> (New York: Schirmer, 1982), p. 499.
    <u>Earth Saga</u> and <u>Lysistrata</u> are unlocated.
21. Program notes titled "Interpretative Spanish Dances"
    performed at the Congregational House, Evanston,
    Illinois. These and other program notes are in the
    American University Archives.
22. Esther Ballou, "Class in Music." Typewritten script,
    American University Archives.
23. Shaffer, p. 3.
24. Tory Baker, interview with Esther Ballou, Chevy Chase,
    Maryland, 21 April 1962.
25. "Angna Enters Program for Derby Connecticut, 13 November
    1942," in American University Archives.
26. Smith, interview, 28 March 1962.
27. In a note to Lloyd Ultan, composer and educator, Ballou
    mentions that the innovative ideas and theories about
    teaching that she used at American University during
    the 1960s were ones that in her words, "I had already
    practiced for some years at Juilliard, even before
    [William] Schuman introduced the new programs there,
    and this was the reason that I was the one person he
    kept on the theory faculty when he became the President
    of Juilliard." Esther Ballou to Lloyd Ultan, December
    31, 1964, American University Archives.

28. Meryle Secrest, "From 8 Hands to Hands by the Dozen:
    'Beguine' to Bow at Youth Concert." Washington Post (8
    October 1962), p. B4.
29. Ibid., p. B4.
30. Middlebury College, "Composers Conference" brochure,
    1949.
31. Secrest, p. B4.
32. Baker, interview, 21 April 1962.
33. "Ballou, Esther Williamson," Two Thousand Women of
    Achievement (London: Melrose Press, 1970), p. 49.
34. Smith, interview, 28 March 1962.
35. Paul Hume, "Two Pianists Play Varied Program." Washing-
    ton Post (22 December 1953).
36. Paul Hume, "Phillips Gallery Concert by Composers' Chap-
    ter." Washington Post (9 March 1955), p. 14.
37. Smith, interview, 28 March 1962.
38. Frank Campbell, "Harry McClure Heard in Piano Recital."
    Washington Evening Star (26 November 1955), p. A12.
39. Paul Hume, "Fine Music Presented at Phillips." Washing-
    ton Post (20 March 1956), p. 35.
40. Edward Downes, "Season Opens for Composers Forum." New
    York Times (7 October 1957), p. 22.
41. Wendell Margrave, "Capital Wind Quintet Shows Good
    Control." Washington Evening Star (19 May 1966), p.
    C21.
42. Esther Ballou, "Theory with a Thrust." Music Educators
    Journal 55/1 (September 1968): 56-57.
43. Mrs. Haywood, Educational TV series, Washington, D.C, 12
    November 1961.
44. "Washington Composer Honored at White House." Washington
    Post (7 September 1963), p. E8.
45. Gordon Smith, interview with Ivan Romenenko, Washington,
    D.C., 19 December 1966.
46. Paul Hume, "National Gallery Concert a Significant Land-
    mark." Washington Post (8 June 1965), p. B6.
47. Esther Ballou, hand-written note, American University
    Archives.
48. Gordon Smith, interview with Esther Ballou, Washington,
    D.C. 17 October 1966.
49. The work was never published.
50. Letter from Patricia Nixon to EWB, 25 June 1971.
51. Letter from Charles Crowder to EWB, 6 February 1972.
52. Joan Reinthaler, "Phillips Concerts: For Elmira Bier."
    Washington Post (12 June 1972), p. B7.
53. Esther Ballou, "Sabbatical Plan," typescript, American
    University Archives.
54. Letter from EWB to Lloyd Ultan, 25 November 1972,
55. "Esther Ballou." Brochure (New York: Broadcast Music,
    Inc., 1968).
56. Baker, interview, 21 April 1962.
57. Robert Parris, "A Composer Reports from Washington."
    Bulletin. American Composers Alliance 7/3 (1958), p.
    8.

58. Note from Lloyd Ultan to William M. Wiebenga, Dean of the
    College of Arts and Sciences, American University, 2
    November 1971, American University Archives.

Works and Performances

"See" references identify citations in the "Bibliography" section (e.g., See: B54), the "Correspondence" section (e.g., See: C29), and "Appendix II: Interviews and Other Audio Sources" (e.g., See: A7). Unless otherwise noted, all manuscripts are located in the American University Archives. ACA publications are available from American Composers Alliance, 170 West 74th Street, New York, N.Y., 10023.

I.   ORCHESTRAL MUSIC

W1.   ADAGIO FOR BASSOON AND STRING ORCHESTRA (1960; ACA; 3 min.)

      Bassoon/strings.
      Composed in Chevy Chase, Maryland.

      Selected performance

W1a.   1974 (Oct 16): Bennington, Vermont; Bennington College; Maurice Pachman, bassoon; 9 string players. See: A7

W2.   BEGUINE FOR ORCHESTRA (1960; ACA; 3 min.) See: B54

      2.2.2.2./4.3.3.1/hp/perc/strings.
      Composed in Chevy Chase, Maryland.
      Originally for two pianos (four pianists). See: W56
      Arranged also for two pianos (two pianists). See: W48

      Premiere

W2a.   1962 (Oct 9): Washington, D.C.; National Symphony
        Orchestra; Howard Mitchell, conductor. <u>See</u>:
        B128, B188

    <u>Other selected performances</u>

W2b.   1962 (Oct 10): Washington, D.C.; National Sympho-
        ny Orchestra; Howard Mitchell, conductor. <u>See</u>:
        B128, B188

W2c.   1963 (Jan 7): Washington,D.C.; National Symphony
        Orchestra; Lloyd Geisler, conducting.

W3.   <u>BLUES FOR ORCHESTRA</u> (1944; manuscript; 3 min.)

        2.2.2.2./4.3.2./perc/strings.
        Composed in New York City.

W4.   <u>CONCERTO FOR PIANO</u> (1945; manuscript; unfinished)

        2 (1 pic).2 (1 Eng hn).2.1/4.3.2.0/pn/perc/timp/
        strings
        Movement I: "Very deliberately."

W5.   <u>CONCERTO FOR PIANO</u> (1965; ACA; 35 min.) <u>See</u>: B69,
       B95; C29

        2 (1 pic).2.1.2/4.2.2.1./timp/perc/pn/strings.
        Completed August 10, 1964.
        Commissioned for the 1000th Concert by the National
           Gallery of Art.
        Dedicated to Hood College.
        Revision (1967) in American University Archives.
        Arranged for two pianos (1965; manuscript)

        <u>Premiere</u>

    W5a.   1965 (Jun 6): Washington,D.C.; National Gallery
            of Art; Charles, Crowder, piano; National Gal-
            lery of Art Orchestra; Richard Bales, conduc-
            tor. <u>See</u>: B105, B165, B205

W6.   <u>CONCERTO FOR PIANO</u> (1972; manuscript; unfinished)

        2.2 (1 Eng. hn).2.2 (1 con bs)/4.3.2.1/timp/perc/
        pn/strings.
        Includes first movement only.
        Composed in Felpham, Bognor Regis, England.
        Commissioned by the British National Youth Orches-
        tra.

W7.   <u>CONCERTO FOR SOLO GUITAR AND CHAMBER ORCHESTRA</u> (1964;
      ACA; 12 min)

      1.1.1.1./1.1.1.0 (optional strings).
      Composed in Chevy Chase, Maryland.
      Composed for Robert Luse.
      <u>Premiere</u>

 W7a.   1964 (May 22): Washington, D.C.; American Univer-
         sity; Robert Luse, guitar; American University
         Orchestra; Thomas Hill, conductor. <u>See</u>: B56

      <u>Other selected performance</u>

 W7b.   1965 (Mar 21): Arlington, Virginia; Unitarian
         Church; Robert Luse, guitar; Members of the
         National Gallery Orchestra; Richard Bales,
         conductor. <u>See</u>: B61, B139

W8.   <u>EARLY AMERICAN PORTRAIT</u> (1962; ACA; 20 min.)

      1 soprano/2 (1 pic).1.1.1/2.1.1.0/perc/hp/strings.
      Composed in Chevy Chase, Maryland.
      Dedicated to Margaret Richards Pabst.
      From "American Frontier," words by Elizabeth S.
        Peck.
      Arranged also for soprano and piano. <u>See</u>: W90

      <u>Selected performance</u>

 W8a.   1965 (Mar 21): Arlington, Virginia; Unitarian
         Church; Katherine Hansel, soprano; Members of
         the National Gallery Orchestra; Richard Bales,
         conductor. <u>See</u>: B61, B139, B167

W9.   <u>IN MEMORIAM FOR OBOE AND STRING ORCHESTRA</u> (1960; ACA;
      5 min.) <u>See</u>: B52; A2

      Oboe/strings.
      Composed in Chevy Chase, Maryland.
      Dedicated to Walter Penland.
      Originally Movement II from <u>Oboe Concertino for
        String Orchestra and Oboe</u>. <u>See</u>: W12

      <u>Premiere</u>

 W9a.   1960 (Apr 3): Washington, D.C.; National Gallery
         of Art; Beth Sears, oboe; National Gallery Or-
         chestra; Richard Bales, conductor. <u>See</u>: B36,
         B140, B161

Other selected performances

W9b.   1960 (May 19): Washington, D.C.; American Univer-
        sity; Gerald Cotts, oboe; American University
        Orchestra; George Steiner, conductor. See:
        B34, B114, B157

W9c.   1965 (Mar 21): Arlington, Virginia; Unitarian
        Church; Beth Sears, oboe; Members of the
        National Gallery Orchestra; Richard Bales,
        conductor. See: B61, B139

W10. INTERMEZZO FOR ORCHESTRA (1943; ACA; 10 min.)

        2.2.2.2/4.2.0.0/strings.
        Composed in New York City.

        Premiere

W10a.   1943 (May 1): New York City; orchestra unknown;
        C. Callinicos, conductor.

W11. KONZERTSTÜCK FOR VIOLA AND ORCHESTRA (1969; ACA; 10
      min.)

        2.2.2.2/4.3.2.1/vla/perc/timp/strings.
        Composed in Chevy Chase, Maryland.
        Composed for and dedicated to Walter Trampler.

W12. OBOE CONCERTINO FOR STRING ORCHESTRA AND OBOE (1953;
      ACA; 12 min.) See: B52, B69

        Oboe/strings.
        Composed in Bennington, Vermont.
        Completed August 22, 1953.
        Movement II later arranged as In Memoriam for Oboe
        and String Orchestra. See: W9

        Premiere

W12a.   1954 (Mar 21): Washington, D.C.; Phillips Gal-
        lery; Walter Penland, oboe; Olevsky Chamber
        Orchestra; Paul Olevsky, conductor. See: B40,
        B199, B201

W13. PRELUDE AND ALLEGRO FOR STRING ORCHESTRA AND PIANO
      (1951; ACA; 7 min.) See: B69, B95, B148, B151,
      B165

        Piano/strings.

Premieres

W13a.   1951 (Aug): Middlebury, Vermont; Composers' Con-
         ference; Esther Ballou, piano; Alan Carter,
         conductor.

W13b.   1953 (Jan 4): Washington, D.C.; Phillips Gallery;
         Esther Ballou, piano; Olefsky Chamber Orches-
         tra; Paul Olefsky, conductor. See: B38, B98,
         B182

Other selected performances

W13c.   1959 (Dec 4): Washington, D.C.; Friday Morning
         Music Club; Evelyn Swarthout, piano; F.M.M.C.
         Ensemble; Emerson Meyers, conductor. See: B50

W13d.   1959 (Jan 16): New York City; Cooper Union; or-
         chestra unknown; Howard Shanet, conductor.
         See: B48

W13e.   1965 (Mar 21): Arlington, Virginia; Unitarian
         Church; Esther Ballou, piano; Members of the
         National Gallery Orchestra; Richard Bales, con-
         ductor. See: B61, B139

W13f.   1968 (May 3): Washington, D.C.; Friday Morning
         Music Club, Barker Hall, Y.W.C.A.; Evelyn
         Swarthout, piano; Friday Morning Music Club
         Instrumental Ensemble; George Steiner, direc-
         tor.

W14.   SUITE FOR CHAMBER ORCHESTRA (1939; manuscript; 4
       min.)

       1.1.0.0./pn/strings.
       Derived from Madchen in Uniform (manuscript unlo-
         cated). See: W107
       Composed at Mills College, Oakland, California.

W15.   SUITE FOR SOLO GUITAR AND STRING ORCHESTRA (no date;
       photocopy of manuscript; 6 min.)

       Guitar/strings.
       Movement I only.
       Original manuscript unlocated.

II. CHAMBER MUSIC

W16. <u>ALLEGRO (IN FIRST POSITION) FOR STRING QUARTET</u> (1943;
      manuscript; 6 min.)

      Composed in New York City.
      Arranged in 1960 for optional string orchestra, in-
      cluding double bass.

W17. <u>BLUES</u> (1930s?; manuscript; 2 min.)

      Clarinet/piano.

W18. <u>BRASS SEXTETTE WITH PIANOFORTE</u> (1962; ACA; 10 min.)

      Trumpet (2)/horn (2)/trombone (2)/piano.
      Composed in Chevy Chase, Maryland.
      Written "for B[ram] Smith."

W19. <u>CAPRICCIO FOR VIOLIN AND PIANO</u> (1963; ACA; 10 min.)
      <u>See</u>: B73; C19

      Composed in Chevy Chase, Maryland.
      Commissioned by the District of Columbia Federation
      of Music Clubs.

      <u>Premieres</u>

W19a. 1963 (Sep 6): Washington, D.C.; The White House;
       Elaine Skorodin, violin; Stephen Prussing,
       piano. <u>See</u>: B31, B55, B84, B119, B133, B137,
       B207

W19b. 1967 (Sep 19): New York City; Town Hall; Ivan
       Romanenko, violin; pianist not cited.

      <u>Other selected performances</u>

W19c. 1964 (Apr 24): Washington, D.C.; Powell Auditori-
       um; Nancy Ellsworth, violin; Esther Ballou,
       piano. <u>See</u>: B56

W19d. 1965 (Apr 22): Washington, D.C.; American Univer-
       sity; Nancy Ellsworth, violin; Esther Ballou,
       piano. <u>See</u>: B88

W19e. 1966 (Dec 19): Washington, D.C.; Phillips Gal-
       lery; Ivan Romanenko, violin; Joan Singer,
       piano. <u>See</u>: B102, B204, A6

W19f. 1970 (Apr 24): Washington, D.C.; American Univer-
       sity; Nancy Mandel, violin; Esther Ballou,
       piano.

W19g.   1978 (Apr 10): Washington, D.C.; American Univer-
         sity; Judith Shapiro, violin; Charles Timbrell,
         piano. See: B57

W19h.   1979 (Apr 27): Washington, D.C.; American
         University; Nancy Ellsworth, violin; Evelyn
         Swarthout, piano.

W19i.   1984 (Mar 4): Washington, D.C.; Mount Vernon Col-
         lege; Melissa Graybeal, violin; Alice Takemoto,
         piano.

W20. CHRISTMAS VARIATIONS FOR RECORDER OR OBOE AND HARPSI-
      CHORD (1954; manuscript; 4 min.) See: C7

      "For P.S. and G.S."

W21. DIALOGUES FOR OBOE AND GUITAR (1966; ACA; 6 min.)

         Movement I based on Movement I of Discussion of
         'Maan'. See: W22
         Revision (June 1969) in American University
         Archives.
         Dedicated to Earnest Harrison.

         Premiere

W21a.   1969 (Apr 11): Baton Rouge, Louisiana; School of
         Music, Louisiana State University; Earnest
         Harrison, oboe; Glenn Caluda, guitar. (26th
         Festival of Contemporary Music) See: B168

         Other selected performance

W21b.   1978 (Apr 10): Washington, D.C.; American Univer-
         sity; Charles Kopfstein-Penk, flute; John
         Marlow, guitar. See: B57

W22. DISCUSSION OF 'MAAN' FOR OBOE AND GUITAR (1966; manu-
      script; 3 min.)

         Movement I revised as movement I of Dialogues for
         Oboe and Guitar. See: W21

W23. DIVERTIMENTO FOR STRING QUARTET (1958; ACA; 10 min.)

      Composed in Chevy Chase, Maryland.

      Premiere

W23a.   1958 (May 11): Washington, D.C.; Phillips Gal-
        lery; American University Quartet; George
        Steiner, violin; Donald Radding, violin;
        Richard Parnas, viola; Morris Kirshbaum, vio-
        loncello. See: B29, B46, B87

        Other selected performances

W23b.   1958 (Nov 16): Washington, D.C.; Catholic Univer-
        sity of America; Members of Sigma Alpha Iota
        and Phi Mu Alpha. See: B97

W23c.   1984 (Mar 14): Washington, D.C.; British Embassy;
        Manchester String Quartet; Hyun-Woo Kim,
        violin; Holly Hamilton, violin; Lynne Edelson
        Levine, viola; Glenn Garlick, violoncello.

W23d.   1984 (May 6): Washington, D.C.; National Gallery
        of Art; Manchester String Quartet; Hyun-Woo
        Kim, violin; Holly Hamilton, violin; Lynne
        Edelson Levine, viola; Glenn Garlick,
        violoncello.

W24.   FANTASIA BREVIS FOR OBOE AND STRINGS (1950; ACA; 2
       min.)

       Composed in New York City.

       Premieres

W24a.   1952 (Aug 13): Greenwood Music Camp. See: B37

W24b.   1953 (Mar 1): New York City: Bennington Compo-
        sers' Conference; Kaufmann Auditorium of the
        Y.M.Y.W.H.; Robert Bloom, oboe; Mary E. Jones,
        violin; Sonya Monosoff, violin; A. Purcell,
        violin; Nellis Delay, violoncello; Lucien
        Laporte, violoncello. See: B38, B158

W25.   FANTASIA BREVIS NO. II FOR OBOE AND STRING QUARTET
       (1952; ACA; 3 min.)

       Dedicated to Robert and Mini Bloom and their
       daughter Katherine.

       Premiere

W25a.   1953 (Mar 1): New York City: Bennington Compo-
        sers' Conference; Kaufmann Auditorium of the
        Y.M.Y.W.H.; Robert Bloom, oboe; Mary E. Jones,
        violin; Sonya Monosoff, violin; A. Purcell,

violin; Nellis Delay, violoncello; Lucien
Laporte, violoncello. See: B38, B183

W26. 5-4-3 (1966; ACA; 14 min.) See: B79, B108, B191; C34

Mezzo-contralto/viola/harp.
"Five" songs "for" "three" performers.
Commissioned by the Kindler Foundation.
Words by e.e.cummings: All which isn't singing is
mere talking/Who is this dainty. . ./May i be
gay/A great/!hope.
First lines: "all which isn't singing is mere talking'; "who is this dainty mademoiselle"; "may i
be gay like every lark"; a great man is gone";
"!hope faith! !life love!"

Premiere

W26a. 1966 (Jun 12): Washington, D.C.; Textile Museum;
Rilla Mervine, mezzo-contralto; Richard Parnas,
viola; Sylvia Meyer, harp. See: B62, B131,
B132, B191

Other selected performances

W26b. 1966 (Oct 17): Washington, D.C.; Phillips Gal-
lery; Rilla Mervine, mezzo-contralto; Richard
Parnas, viola; Faith Carman, harp. See: B111,
B186, A5

W26c. 1973 (Oct 28): Washington, D.C.; Phillips Gallery; Rilla Mervine, mezzo-contralto; Frank
Conlon, piano. See: B175

W26d. 1974 (Oct 16): Bennington, Vermont; Bennington
College; Richard Frisch, vocal; Jacob Glick,
viola; Susan Jolles, harp. See: A7

W26e. 1978 (Apr 10): Washington, D.C.; American University; Elizabeth Kirkpatrick, soprano; Cynthia
Kitt, viola; Sylvia Sanders, harp. See: B57

W27. HAIKU (1968; manuscript; 2 min.)

Soprano/tape/flute/clarinet/violin.
Text: "oo-ah--The bird flew on leaving behind only
the sound of the wind."
Composed in Chevy Chase, Maryland.

W28. IMPERTINENCE FOR CLARINET AND PIANO (1936; manuscript; 2 min.)

Composed in Bennington, Vermont.
Arranged also for two pianos. <u>See</u>: W58

<u>Premiere</u>

W28a.   1936 (Nov 7): New York City; WABC Radio; Robert
McBride, clarinet; Esther Ballou, piano. <u>See</u>:
B70

W29. <u>IN BLUES TEMPO</u> (1937; manuscript; 2 min.)

Clarinet/piano.
Arranged also for piano (four hands). <u>See</u>: W60

W30. <u>LAMENT FOR VIOLONCELLO AND PIANO</u> (1945; manuscript; 4
min.)

Later included as first movement in <u>Suite for Violoncello and Piano</u> (1951). <u>See</u>: W38

W31. <u>LET-DOWN FOR OBOE OR VIOLIN AND PIANO</u> (1937; manuscript; 2 min.)

"For Robert McBride."

W32. <u>MINUTIAE FOR FLUTE AND PIANO</u> (1953; manuscript; 2
min.)

"For Otto" [Luening].

W33. <u>NOCTURNE FOR STRING QUARTET</u> (1937; manuscript; 3
min.)

<u>Selected performance</u>

W33a.   1976 (Apr 9): Washington, D.C.; Kennedy Center
for the Performing Arts; Friday Morning Music
Club Instrumental Ensemble; Jerzy Sapieyevski,
director. <u>See</u>: B24

W34. <u>A PLAINTIVE NOTE</u> [and] <u>A CHEERFUL NOTE</u> (1951; ACA; 4
min.)

Violoncello/piano.
Composed in Wilmington, Vermont.
Dedicated to Julian DeGray.

W35.   PRIDE, ENVY, SLOTH, LUST, ANGER (1960; manuscript; 4
       min.)

       Soprano/piano/percussion.

W36.   PRISM FOR STRING TRIO (1969; ACA; 14 min.)

       Violin/viola/violoncello/tape.
       Revision (Nov 1969) in American University Ar-
          chives.
       Composed in Chevy Chase, Maryland.
       Dedicated to the Potomac Trio.

       Premieres

W36a.   1969 (Oct 25): Washington, D.C.; Barker Hall,
         Y.W.C. A.; Potomac Trio; Judith Shapiro,
         violin; Melissa Graybeal, viola; Thea Cooper,
         violoncello. See: B169

W36b.   1970 (Feb 13): New York City; Carnegie Hall;
         Potomac Trio; Judith Shapiro, violin; Melissa
         Graybeal, viola; Thea Cooper, violoncello.

       Other selected performances

W36c.   1970 (Feb 16): Norfolk, Virginia; Norfolk Museum;
         Potomac Trio; Judith Shapiro, violin; Melissa
         Graybeal, viola; Thea Cooper, violoncello.

W36d.   1973 (Mar 28): Washington, D.C.; American Univer-
         sity; Potomac Trio; Judith Shapiro, violin;
         Melissa Graybeal, viola; Dorothy Jarvinen, vio-
         loncello.

W36e.   1973 (Apr 4): Wellesley College; Potomac Trio;
         Judith Shapiro, violin; Melissa Graybeal, vio-
         la; Dorothy Jarvinen, violoncello.

W36f.   1978 (Apr 10): Washington, D.C.; American Univer-
         sity; Judith Shapiro, violin; Barbara Winslow,
         viola; Dorothy Jarvinen, violoncello. See: B57

W37.   ROMANZA OR L'HISTOIRE D'UN ROMANCE (1969; ACA; 3
       min.)

       Violin/piano.
       Composed for Ann and Earl Carlyss.
       Composed in Chevy Chase, Maryland.

W38. SUITE FOR VIOLONCELLO AND PIANO (1951; ACA; 7 min.)
      See: B39

      First movement originally Lament for Violoncello
      and Piano (1945). See: W30

W39. SUITE FOR WINDS (1957; ACA; 7 min.) See: A2

      Flutes (2)/oboes (2)/clarinets (2)/ bassoons (2)/
      horns (2).

      Premiere

   W39a. 1957 (Mar): Washington, D.C.; Catholic University
          of America; U.S. Air Force Symphonette; Col.
          George S. Howard, conductor.

      Other selected performances

   W39b. 1957 (May 12): Washington, D.C.; Catholic Univer-
          sity of America; Members of Beta Phi Chapter of
          Sigma Alpha Iota, and Eta Theta Chapter of Phi
          Mu Alpha. See: B28

   W39c. 1958 (Mar 23): Washington, D.C.; Corcoran Gallery
          of Art; U.S. Air Force Symphonette; Col. George
          S. Howard, conductor. See: B46

W40. THEME AND VARIATIONS ON SHENANDOAH ALMA MATER (n.d.;
      manuscript; 3 min.)

      Violin/viola/violoncello/piano.

W41. TRIO FOR VIOLIN, VIOLONCELLO, AND PIANO (1955; ACA;
      15 min.) See: B45

      Composed at the MacDowell Colony, Peterborough, New
      Hampshire.
      Commissioned by the Washington Branch of the
      National American Association of Composers and
      Conductors.
      Revision (1957) in American University Archives.

      Premiere

   W41a. 1956 (Mar 19): Washington, D.C.; Phillips Gal-
          lery; James Barber, violin; John Engberg,
          violoncello; Esther Ballou, piano. See: B43,
          B101, B135

      Other selected performances

W41b.   1957 (Aug 21): Bennington, Vermont; Composers'
        Conference; Max Pollikoff, violin; George
        Finkel, violoncello; Esther Ballou, piano.
        See: B44

W41c.   1957 (Oct 5): New York City; Columbia University;
        Composers Forum; Donald Portnoy, violin; John
        Engberg, violoncello; Gene Akers, piano. See:
        B1, B35, B44, B67

W41d.   1958 (Oct 12): Washington, D.C.; Corcoran Gallery
        of Art; Donald Portnoy, violin; John Engberg,
        violoncello; Gene Akers, piano. See: B134

W41e.   1974 (Jan 18): Washington, D.C.; Barker Hall,
        Y.W.C.A.; Genevieve Fritter, violin; Jean
        Robbins, violoncello; Lydia Bernstein, piano.

W41f.   1974 (Oct 16): Bennington, Vermont; Bennington
        College; Joanna Jenner, violin; Barbara Mallow,
        violoncello; Lionel Nowak, piano. See: A7

W41g.   1977 (Jun 23): Toronto, Canada; Royal Conserva-
        tory of Music; Matthay Festival; Eugene Kash,
        violin; Robert Spergel, violoncello; Earle
        Moss, piano.

W42. UN MORCEAU D'ENSEMBLE SUR LE NOM D'ELMIRA FOR STRING
      QUARTET (1972; manuscript; 4 min.) See: C63, C64

      Composed in Chevy Chase, Maryland.
      Dedicated to Elmira Bier.

      Premiere

W42a.   1972 (Jun 10): Washington, D.C.; Phillips Gal-
        lery; George Steiner, violin; Virginia Harpham,
        violin; Richard Parnas, viola; John Martin,
        violoncello.

      Other selected performance

W42b.   1972 (Jun 11): Washington, D.C.; Phillips Gal-
        lery; George Steiner, violin; Virginia Harpham,
        violin; Richard Parnas, viola; John Martin,
        violoncello. See: B178

W43. VIOLIN AND PIANOFORTE SONATA (1937-38; manuscript; 8
      min.)

      Composed at Mills College, Oakland, California.

Domenico Brescia's name is written on first page of
second movement.

W44.   VIOLIN SONATINA (1959; manuscript; 3 min.)

Violin/piano.
Third movement only.

W45.   WHAT IF A MUCH OF A WHICH OF A WIND (1959; ACA; 12
min.)

Soprano/baritone/bass/flute/oboe/clarinet/bassoon/
horn.
First line: same as title.

Premiere

W45a.   1960 (May 17): Baltimore, Maryland; Baltimore
Museum of Art; Contemporary Wind Ensemble;
Richard Pittman, conductor; Mary Alice Bennet,
soprano; John Yard, baritone; Paul Erickson,
bass.

W46.   WIND QUINTETTE (1953; manuscript; unfinished)

Flute/oboe/clarinet/horn/bassoon.
Movement II only.

III. KEYBOARD MUSIC

W47.   ART OF THE FUGUE: "CONTRAPUNCTUS V [AND] IX." (1963;
manuscript; 5 min.)

Piano (four hands).
An arrangement of J.S. Bach's Art of the Fugue:
"Contrapunctus V [and]IX.

Premiere

W47a.   1963 (Apr 23): Washington, D.C.; American University; Clendenen Hall; Esther Ballou and Evelyn
Swarthout, duo-pianos. See: B89

W48.   BEGUINE FOR TWO PIANOS (1957; ACA; 3 min.) See: B94

Originally for two pianos (four pianists). <u>See</u>:
W56
Arranged also for orchestra. <u>See</u>: W2

<u>Selected performances</u>

W48a. 1958 (Apr 18): Washington, D.C.; Cosmos Club
       Assembly Hall; Alice and Arthur Nagle, duo-
       pianos. <u>See</u>: B46

W48b. 1958 (Apr 27): Washington, D.C.; Music Room of
       Mrs. Anne Archbold; Alice and Arthur Nagle,
       duo-pianos. <u>See</u>: B46

W48c. 1984 (Nov 24): Washington, D.C.; The Pavilion at
       the Old Post Office; Leanne Rees and Stephanie
       Stoyanoff, duo-pianos.

W49. <u>BERCEUSE FOR PIANO</u> (1956; manuscript; 1 min.)

W50. <u>BROWN ORCHIDS</u> (1942; manuscript; 1 min.)

      Piano.
      "To Betty."

W51. <u>CHROMATIC INVENTION</u> (n.d.; manuscript; 2 min.)

      Piano (four hands).
      Not signed by Ballou, but likely her composition.

W52. <u>COUNTRY DANCE FOR PIANO</u> (1937; manuscript; 2 min.)

      "Rondo"; "Form ABACABA."

W53. <u>DANCE SUITE</u> (1937-61; manuscript; 6 min.)

      Piano.
      Prelude (1953)/Rigaudon (1937)/Sarabande (1961;
       ACA)/Galliarde (1937)/Courante (1937)/Bouree
       (1937)/Gigue (1937).

      <u>Selected performances</u>

W53a. 1961 (Nov 12): Washington, D.C.; childrens
       series, public broadcasting television; Esther
       Ballou, piano; "Rigaudon" and "Gigue" only.
       <u>See</u>: A1

W53b.   1974 (May 12): Rockville, Maryland; Montgomery
College; Sean Breen, piano.

W53c.   1981 (Mar 8): Jersey City, New Jersey; The
Sisters at 78 Grand Street; Sister Rosalie
McQuaide, piano; "Prelude" (1953) and
"Sarabande" (1961) only.

W54.   <u>11 PIANO TEACHING PIECES</u> (1950s; ACA; 6 min.)

Piano.
"Before the Party"/"My Scooter"/"Busy-Body"/"Copy-
Cat"/"Johnnie's Donkey"/"Bubble-Gum (It
Stretches, then Pops!)"/"Mozart in Five"/"The
Dance of the Wooden Shoes"/"Dreams"/"Go to
Sleep"/"The Alarm Clock."

W55.   <u>FOR ART NAGLE ON HIS BIRTHDAY</u> (1968; manuscript; 2
min.)

Piano.
Composed in Chevy Chase, Maryland.

W56.   <u>FORTY FINGER BEGUINE FOR TWO PIANOS</u> (1950; ACA; 3
min.)

Two pianos (four pianists).
Arranged in 1957 for two pianos (two pianists).
<u>See</u>: W48
Arranged in 1960 for orchestra. <u>See</u>: W2

<u>Premiere</u>

W56a.   1951 (Mar): Washington, D.C.(?)

<u>Other selected performance</u>

W56b.   1974 (Oct 16): Bennington, Vermont; Bennington
College; Vivian Fine, David Levine, Marianne
Finckel, Phyllis Pearson, pianists. <u>See</u>: A7

W57.   <u>FOUR-HAND SUITE</u> (1957; manuscript, unfinished; 4
min.)

Piano (four hands).
Movement I only.

W58.   <u>IMPERTINENCE FOR TWO PIANOS</u> (1936; manuscript; 2
min.)

Composed in Bennington, Vermont.
Originally for clarinet and piano. See: W28

W59.   IMPROMPTU FOR ORGAN (1968; ACA; 2 min.)

Composed in Chevy Chase, Maryland.
"For Dr. Rockholr."

Selected performance

W59a.   1980 (Jul 27): Washington, D.C.; Christ Lutheran
Church; Geoffrey Simon, organ.

W60.   IN BLUES TEMPO (1937; manuscript; 2 min.)

Piano (four hands).
Arranged also for clarinet and piano. See: W29

W61.   JAZZ THEME AND VARIATIONS (1936; manuscript; 3 min.)

Piano.
"Blues"/"Fox Trot"/"Waltz."

W62.   MUSIC FOR THE THEATRE (1951; manuscript; 5 min.)

Two pianos.
Composed in Washington, D.C.

W63.   OVERTURE "OF THEE I SING" (1930s; manuscript; 5 min.)

Two pianos.
An arrangement of George Gershwin's "Of Thee I
Sing."
Ballou's name not on manuscript.

Premiere

W63a.   1937 (Jun 6): New York; Esther Ballou, piano;
other pianist not known.

W64.   PASSACAGLIA AND TOCCATA FOR ORGAN (1962; ACA; 9 min.)

Written for Harlan Laufman.
Dedicated to Marta Mercey.

Premiere

W64a.   1963 (Mar 15): Washington, D.C.; St. Thomas Epis-
         copal Church; Harlan Laufman, organ.

Other selected performances

W64b.   1963 (Oct 6): Washington, D.C.; Washington
         National Cathedral; Katherine Eskey, organ.
         See: B55

W64c.   1964 (Nov 9): Washington, D.C.; St. Thomas Epis-
         copal Church; Harlan Laufman, organ.

W64d.   1965 (Mar 1): Washington, D.C.; American Guild of
         Organists; St. Thomas Episcopal Church; Harlan
         Laufman, organ.

W64e.   1967 (May): Washington, D.C.; Metropolitan Memo-
         rial Methodist Church; Margaret Scharf, organ.

W65. PIECE FOR PIANO (UNTITLED) (1960s; manuscript; 2
      min.)

      A composition for unusual effects on the strings by
      using the fingers and a mallet.

W66. PORTRAIT I (1968; manuscript; 1 min.)

      Piano.

W67. PRELUDE AND GIGUE FOR PIANO (1948; manuscript; 3
      min.)

W68. PRELUDES FOR PIANO (1940-41; manuscript; 4 min.)

      Includes five preludes.
      Composed at the Juilliard Graduate School, N.Y.C.

W69. PRELUDE NUMBER 1, 2, and 3 FOR PIANO (1939; manu-
      script; 3 min.)

W70. PRELUDE I FOR PIANO (1960; manuscript; 2 min.)

W71. RONDINO FOR HARPSICHORD (1961; manuscript; 3 min.)
      See: B54

      Written for Robert Parris.

Premiere

W71a.   1962 (Jan 1): Washington, D.C.; Phillips Gallery;
         Robert Parris, harpsichord. See: B112, B150

W72. SONATA FOR PIANO (1954; ACA; 13 min.) See: B93,
      B179; A2

      Composed at the MacDowell Colony.
      Corrections made by the composer on manuscript in
      American University Archives.

      Premiere

W72a.   1955 (Mar 7): Washington, D.C.; Phillips Gallery;
         Esther Ballou, piano. See: B41, B106, B144

      Other selected performances

W72b.   1955 (Nov 25): Washington, D.C.; Corcoran Gallery
         of Art; Harry McClure, piano. See: B30, B42

W72c.   1956 (Aug 12): Bennington, Vermont; Bennington
         Composers' Conference; Lionel Nowak, piano.
         See: B43

W72d.   1956 (Dec 4): College Park, Maryland; University
         of Maryland; Stewart Gordon, piano.

W72e.   1957 (Feb 14): Washington, D.C.; Arts Club; Harry
         McClure, piano. See: B27

W72f.   1957 (Oct 5): New York City; Columbia University;
         Composers Forum; Lionel Nowak, piano. See: B1,
         B35, B44

W72g.   1958 (Nov 2): Washington, D.C.; Phillips Gallery;
         Helen McGraw, piano. See: B110, B141

W72h.   1960 (May 18): Washington, D.C.; American Univer-
         sity; Richard D. Ringenwald, piano. See: B179

W72i.   1964 (Apr 24): Washington, D.C.; Powell Auditori-
         um; Maria Stoesser, piano. See: B56

W72j.   1968 (Jan 17): Washington, D.C.; American Univer-
         sity; Alan Mandel, piano.

W72k.   1968 (Jan 21): Washington, D.C.; National Gallery
         of Art; Alan Mandel, piano. See: B176

W73. <u>SONATA FOR TWO PIANOS</u> (1949; New York: Mercury Music;
      14 min.) <u>See</u>: B43, B94

      "To H.S."
      Revision (1969) in American University Archives.

      <u>Premiere</u>

 W73a.   1953 (Dec 21): Washington, D.C.; Phillips
         Gallery; Esther Ballou and Harry McClure, duo-
         pianos. <u>See</u>: B39, B116, B200

      <u>Other selected performances</u>

 W73b.   1970 (Feb 6): Washington, D.C.; Barker Hall;
         Y.W.C.A.; Esther Ballou and Charles Crowder,
         duo-pianos.

 W73c.   1970 (Oct 24): Washington, D.C.; Catholic Univer-
         sity; Province Day, Sigma Alpha Iota; Esther
         Ballou and Charles Crowder, duo-pianos.

 W73d.   1976 (Feb 28): Washington, D.C.; American Univer-
         sity; Evelyn Swarthout and Charles Crowder,
         duo-pianos.

 W73e.   1977 (Jun 23): Toronto, Canada; Royal Conserva-
         tory of Music; Matthay Festival; Evelyn
         Swarthout and Milton Kidd, duo-pianos.

 W73f.   1978 (Apr 10): Washington, D.C.; American Univer-
         sity; Suzanne Baker and Milton Kidd, duo-
         pianos. <u>See</u>: B57

W74. <u>SONATA FOR TWO PIANOS NO. 2</u> (1958; ACA; 14 min.)

      "To Alice and Arthur Nagle."
      Composed in Chevy Chase, Maryland.

      <u>Premiere</u>

 W74a.   1959 (Aug 8): San Francisco; Sigma Alpha Iota
         National Convention; Margaret Ann McConnell and
         Carolyn Osborne, duo-pianos. <u>See</u>: B49, B190

      <u>Other selected performances</u>

 W74b.   1959 (Oct 13): Cedar Falls, Iowa; Iowa State
         Teachers College; Alice and Arthur Nagle, duo-
         pianos. <u>See</u>: B

W74c.   1960 (Mar 20): Washington, D.C.; Catholic Univer-
         sity of America; Alice and Arthur Nagle, duo-
         pianos. See: B5

W74d.   1976 (Feb 23): Washington, D.C.; Kennedy Center
         for the Performing Arts; Alice and Arthur
         Nagle, duo-pianos. See: B66

W74e.   1986 (Apr 13): Washington, D.C.; Corcoran Gallery
         of Art; Leanne Rees and Stephanie Stoyanoff,
         duo-pianos.

W75. SONATINA (1941; manuscript; 4 min.)

         Piano.

W76. SONATINA NO. 2 (1964; manuscript; 3 min.)

         Piano.
         Commissioned by the Music Teachers National Associ-
         ation.
         Composed in Chevy Chase, Maryland.

         Selected performance

   W76a.   1974 (May 12): Rockville, Maryland; Montgomery
            College; Marcia Kozub, piano.

W77. A TELEPHONE NUMBER (1960s; manuscript; 30 sec.)

         Piano.
         "To ESH [Evelyn Swarthout Hayes] from EWB."

W78. TRIUMPHANT FIGURE (1960s; manuscript; 3 min.)

         Piano.
         Manuscript unlocated.
         Cited in B71.

W79. VARIATIONS FOR GAIL (1964; manuscript; 3 min.)

         Piano.
         Five variations plus coda.

W80. VARIATIONS, SCHERZO AND FUGUE ON A THEME BY LOU
      HARRISON (1959; ACA; 13 min.) See: B93; A2

         Piano.

Theme based on Sonata No. 1 from Six Cembalo
Sonatas (1935-40) by Lou Harrison.
Dedicated to the Friday Morning Music Club 75th
Anniversary.
Composed for Evelyn Swarthout.

Premiere

W80a.   1960 (Mar 26): Washington, D.C.; Friday Morning
Music Club; Evelyn Swarthout, piano. See: B51

Other selected performances

W80b.   1960 (May 3): Washington, D.C.; Corcoran Gallery
of Art; Evelyn Swarthout, piano. See: B143

W80c.   1960 (May 9): Washington, D.C.; American University; Evelyn Swarthout, piano.

W80d.   1963 (May 9): New Haven, Connecticut; Southern
Connecticut State College; Selma Epstein,
piano. See: B55

W80e.   1964 (Jul 27): Washington, D.C.; American University; Evelyn Swarthout, piano. See: B56

W80f.   1964 (Aug 2): Andover, Mass.; Phillips Academy;
Evelyn Swarthout, piano. See: B56, B59

W80g.   1967 (Jan 15): College Park, Maryland; University
of Maryland; Stewart Gordon, piano. See: B206

W80h.   1969 (Mar 26): Washington, D.C.; American University; Evelyn Swarthout, piano. See: B115, B187

W80i.   1972 (Apr 3): Virgin Islands; St. Thomas;
Constant Great House; Evelyn Swarthout, piano.
See: B77

W80j.   1972 (Apr 16): Pittsburgh; Chatham College;
Evelyn Swarthout, piano.

W80k.   1972 (Apr 30): Washington, D.C.; Kennedy Center
for the Performing Arts; Evelyn Swarthout,
piano. See: B127, B130, B174

W80l.   1973 (Mar 28): Washington, D.C.; American University; Evelyn Swarthout, piano.

W80m.   1974 (Jan 18): Washington, D.C.; Barker Hall;
Y.W.C.A.; Evelyn Swarthout, piano.

W80n.   1974 (May 12): Rockville, Maryland; Montgomery
College; Deborah Braun, piano.

W80o.   1975 (Apr 26): Washington, D.C.; Barker Hall;
        Y.W.C.A.; Evelyn Swarthout, piano.

W80p.   1977 (Jun 23): Toronto, Canada; Royal Conserva-
        tory of Music; Matthay Festival; Evelyn
        Swarthout, piano.

W80q.   1984 (Feb 12): Washington, D.C.; Wesley United
        Methodist Church; Bonnie Kellert, piano.

W80r.   1986 (Apr 20): Washington, D.C.; National Gallery
        of Art; Alice Takemoto, piano.

IV.   OTHER SOLO INSTRUMENTAL MUSIC

W81.   ELEGY FOR SOLO CELLO (1968; manuscript; 7 min.)

       Written in memory of Marian Davis.

       Premiere

W81a.   1969 (May 4): Washington, D.C.; Phillips Gallery;
        Ervin Klinkon, violoncello. See: B21, B166

V.   CHORAL MUSIC

W82.   A BABE IS BORN (1959; ACA; 3 min.)

       SATB.
       Words: fifteenth century.
       First line: same as title.

       Premiere

W82a.   1959 (Dec 17): Washington, D.C.; American Univer-
        sity; Clendenen Hall; American University Cho-
        rus; Gordon H. Smith, conductor. See: B50, B65

W83.   BAG OF TRICKS (1956; manuscript; 3 min.)

       Women's voices SSAA.
       Words by Irene Orgel.
       First line: "The conjorer. . . ."

W84. THE BEATITUDES (1957; ACA; 23 min.)

> Soprano solo/alto solo/SATB/organ.
> First line: "Blessed Are the Poor in Spirit."

> Premiere

W84a. 1962 (Nov 17): Washington, D.C.; Metropolitan
>   Memorial Methodist Church; James L. McLain,
>   conductor. See: B55

W85. HEAR US! (1967; Waco, Texas: Word, Inc., 1969; 7
>   min.)

> SATB/organ; optional brass (trumpet (c)/trumpet (B
> flat)/horn/trombone/ ehphonium or tuba.
> Composed for American University on occasion of
>   their 75th Anniversary. See: C46, C48
> First line: "Great God Almighty!"

> Premiere

W85a. 1968 (Feb 24): Washington, D.C.; Metropolitan
>   Memorial Methodist Church; American University
>   Singers; Vito Mason, conductor; Mary Gay Craig,
>   accompanist.

> Other selected performances

W85b. 1968 (Apr 17): Washington, D.C.; Pan American
>   Union; Hall of the Americas; American Universi-
>   ty Singers; Vito Mason, conductor. See: B173

W85c. 1969 (Oct 17): Baltimore; All-Maryland High
>   School Chorus; Vito Mason, conductor; Penelope
>   Hallett, accompanist.

W85d. 1970 (Sep 27): Washington, D.C.; Metropolitan
>   Memorial Methodist Church; American University
>   Singers; Vito Mason, conductor. See: B78, B99

W85e. 1973 (Mar 28): Washington, D.C.; American Univer-
>   sity; Alumni and Friends; Vito Mason, conduc-
>   tor.

W86. I WILL LIFT UP MINE EYES (1965; manuscript; 6 min.)

> Soprano solo/SATB/organ.
> Psalm 121.
> First line: "I Will Lift Up Mine Eyes Unto the
>   Hills."
> Commissioned by Hermann Berlinski.

Composed in Elmira, New York.

<u>Premiere</u>

W86a.   1967 (Feb 24): Washington, D.C.; Washington
        Hebrew Congregation; Combined choral groups of
        the Washington Hebrew Congregation and American
        University; Vito Mason, conductor; Geoffrey
        Simon, organ.

W87. <u>MAY THE WORDS</u> (1965; ACA; 2 min.)

        SATB (a cappella); piano/organ part for rehearsal
        only.
        First line: "May the Words of My Mouth."
        Commissioned by Hermann Berlinski.

        <u>Premiere</u>

W87a.   1967 (Feb 24): Washington, D.C.; Washington
        Hebrew Congregation; Combined choral groups of
        the Washington Hebrew Congregation and American
        University; Vito Mason, conductor.

W88. <u>O THE SUN COMES UP-UP-UP IN THE OPENING</u> (1966; ACA; 3
      min.)

        SSA.
        Words: e.e. cummings.
        First line: "O the sun comes up-up-up in the
        opening sky."
        Commissioned by Sigma Alpha Iota Sorority.

VI. SONGS

W89. <u>BRIDE</u> (1962; ACA; 4 min.)

        Soprano/organ.
        Words by Virginia Sorensen.
        First line: "I Too Weep Cool Deep Tears."
        Commissioned by Jane Krell.

        <u>Selected performance</u>

W89a.   1963 (Feb): New York City; WNYC broadcast; Mary
        Ann Stabile, soprano; Norman Scribner, organ.

W90.   <u>FIVE SONGS FOR SOPRANO</u> (1962; ACA; 20 min.)   <u>See</u>:
         B197

              Soprano/piano.
              Five songs: "Wild Geese"; "The Loiterer";
                 "Buffaloes"; "The Christening"; "Democracy."
              From "American Frontier," words by Elizabeth S.
                 Peck.
              First lines: "Last Night I Heard the Wild Geese
                 Flying Southward"; "My Father's Rule Remained the
                 Same Out West"; "Ten Thousand Farm-Bred Cattle
                 Mild, by Liquor Lured to Clownish Play"; "Little
                 One, You Sleep, and I Keep thinking"; "Pat, Pat.
                 . . ."
              "To the memory of Margaret Richards Pabst."
              "The Loiterer" is an arrangement of "Whip-Poor-
                 Will." <u>See</u>: W101
              Five Songs for Soprano is also arranged as <u>Early</u>
                 <u>American Portrait</u> for soprano and orchestra.
                 <u>See</u>: W8

              <u>Selected performances</u>

W90a.   1964 (Apr 24): Washington, D.C.; Powell Auditori-
              um; Katherine Hansel, soprano; Esther Ballou,
              piano. <u>See</u>: B56

W90b.   1966 (Nov 21): Washington, D.C.; Phillips Gal-
              lery; Jane White, soprano; Sara Klinkon, piano;
              "Buffaloes" not included. <u>See</u>: B103, B185

W90c.   1966 (Dec 12): Washington, D.C.; Phillips Gal-
              lery; Emma Porter, soprano; William Petterson,
              piano; only "Wild Geese," "The Loiterer," and
              and "Buffaloes." <u>See</u>: B5

W90d.   1970 (Jan 16): Washington, D.C.; White House;
              Katherine Hansel, soprano; Esther Ballou,
              piano; "Wild Geese" and "The Loiterer" only.

W90e.   1974 (Jan 18): Washington, D.C.; Barker Hall;
              Y.W.C.A.; Elizabeth Kirkpatrick, soprano;
              Gillian Cookson, piano.

W90f.   1976 (Mar 28): Washington, D.C.; United Church;
              Jane White, soprano; Peggy Kelley Reinburg,
              piano; "The Christening" and "Wild Geese" only.

W90g.   1976 (Nov 21): Washington, D.C.; Phillips Gal-
              lery; Katherine Hansel, soprano; accompanist
              unknown. <u>See</u>: B177

W90h.   1976 (Dec 28): Philadelphia; National Association
              of Teachers Thirty First Convention; Katherine

Hansel, soprano; Edwin Ferguson, piano; "Wild
Geese" and "The Loiterer" only.

W90i.   1977 (Jun 23): Toronto, Canada; Royal Conserva-
tory of Music; Matthay Festival; Elizabeth
Hageman Buls, soprano; Stephen Siek, piano;
"The Loiterer" and "Democracy" only.

W90j.   1977 (Aug 14): Ann Arbor; University of Michigan;
Lorine Summers, soprano; Beth Gilbert, piano.
See: B198

W91. FOUR SONGS (1937; manuscript; 8 min.)

Soprano/piano.
Words from "A Shropshire Lad" by A.E. Housman.
Titles: "Oh, Fair Enough"; "Loveliest of Trees";
"If Truth in Hearts that Perish"; "Look Not in My
Eyes."
First lines: "Oh, Fair Enough are Sky and Plain";
"Loveliest of Trees, the Cherry Now is Hung with
Bloom along the Bough"; "If Truth in Hearts that
Perish"; "Look Not in My Eyes for Fear They
Mirror True."

Premiere

W91a.   1944 (Nov 8): New York City (?); Sylvia Singer,
soprano; Esther Williamson (Ballou), piano;
"Loveliest of Trees" only.

W92. RUMBA ON RIVERSIDE DRIVE (1940s; manuscript; 2 min.)

Miriam Workman, joint composer.
Soprano/piano.
Words by Arthur Herzog, Jr.
First line: "When the Moon Rides over Manhatten."

W93. THE SEA IN MAINE: THE PRESENCE OF THE SEA (1962; manuscript; 3 min.)

Baritone/piano.
Words by Benedict Thielen.
First line: "There is a Motion."
Composed in Stonington, Maine.

W94. THE SHEPHERD (1944; manuscript; 1 min.)

Soprano/piano.
Words by William Blake.

First line: "How Sweet is the Shepherd's Sweet Lot."

<u>Premiere</u>

W94a.   1944 (Nov 8): New York City (?); Sylvia Singer, soprano; Esther Williamson (Ballou), piano.

W95.   <u>A SONG</u> (1938; manuscript; 1 min.)

Mezzo-soprano/piano.
Words by William B. Yeats.
First line: "All the Words that I Utter."

W96.   <u>A SONG</u> (1949; manuscript; 1 min.)

Soprano/piano.
Words by Ben Hamilton.
First line: "The Rippling Waters Play."

W97.   <u>A SONG</u> (1967; ACA; 2 min.)

Alto or mezzo-soprano/piano.
Words by John Ciardi.
First line: "I Want to Tell You a Gentlest Thing."
"On their 25th anniversary--To Helen and Don."

W98.   <u>STREET SCENES</u> (1960; ACA; 7 min.)   <u>See</u>: B55

Soprano/piano.
Four songs: "Summer"; "Autum"; "Winter"; "Spring."
Words by Hansi Champers.
First lines: "Its Summer Time When the City Boy Sees the City Man"; "Like a Bright Young Duchess at an Ancient Rite"; "The Wind Around the Corner Slips"; "Spring Comes Kissing, Kissing, Kissing, Soft and Sweet."
"For Mary Ann Cooper."

<u>Selected performances</u>

W98a.   1961 (Nov 12): Washington, D.C.; childrens series, public broadcasting television; Jeanne Gage, soprano; Esther Ballou, piano. <u>See</u>: A1

W98b.   1977 (Jun 23): Toronto, Canada; Royal Conservatory of Music; Matthay Festival; Elizabeth Hageman Buls, soprano; Stephen Siek, piano.

W98c.   1981 (May 27): Charleston, South Carolina; Col-
         lege of Charleston; Lynne Anders, soprano;
         Haskell Small, piano. <u>See</u>: B146

W98d.   1981 (Nov 1): Washington, D.C.; Chinese Community
         Church; Lynne Anders, soprano; Muriel Hom,
         piano; "Summer" and "Autumn" only.

W98e.   1985 (Apr 16): Washington, D.C.; George Washing-
         ton University; Jennifer A. Limbert, soprano;
         Hae-Ja Yang, piano; "Autumn" only.

W99. <u>TIME</u> (1937; manuscript; 1 min.)

         Soprano/piano.
         Words by Emma Swan.
         First Line: "I Can't Stop Time from Slipping Thru
         My Fingers."

W100. <u>UP INTO THE SILENCE</u> (1968; manuscript; 3 min).

         High soprano/piano.
         Words by e.e. cummings.
         First line: "Up Into the Silence."
         "Composed for the wedding of Helen Fox and Charles
         Crowder."

         <u>Premiere</u>

  W100a.   1968 (Apr 26): Washington, D.C.; St. Margaret's
           Episcopal Church; Katherine Hansel; Paul Hume,
           organ.

         <u>Other selected performance</u>

  W100b.   1973 (Mar 28): Washington, D.C.; American Univer-
           sity; Elizabeth Kirkpatrick, soprano; Geoffrey
           Simon, organ.

W101. <u>WHIP-POOR-WILL</u> (1962; manuscript; 1 min.)

         Soprano/piano.
         From "American Frontier." Words by Elizabeth Peck.
         First line: "My Father's Rule Remained the Same Out
         West."
         Dedicated to Margaret R. Pabst.
         Later revised and renamed "The Loiterer" in <u>Five
         Songs for Soprano</u>. <u>See</u>: W90

VII. MUSIC FOR DANCE, STAGE, AND FILM

W102. ACCOMPANIMENTS FOR MODERN DANCE TECHNIQUE (1933-37;
   manuscript)

    Piano.
    Used in modern dance classes taught by Martha Hill,
     Doris Humphrey, and Bessie Schoenberg.

W103. CLASS IN MUSIC (1940; manuscript; 5 min.)

    2.1.1.1/0.1.1.1.
    Score and script for educational animated film
     starring Mickie and Minnie Mouse.
    Script by Esther Ballou.
    Three scenes: "Class in Music"; "Practice Scenes";
     "Fugue."

W104. EARTH SAGA (1938; manuscript; 10 min.)

    Piano (four hands).
    Choreography by Louise Kloepper.
    Manuscript unlocated.
    Cited in B71.

W105. FUGATO (1960s; manuscript; '4 min.)

    5 winds/3 brass.
    Documentary film.
    Copy unlocated.
    Cited in B71.

W106. LYSISTRATA (1930s; manuscript)

    Composed at Mills College, Oakland, California.
    Choreography by José Limón.
    Score unlocated.

W107. MADCHEN IN UNIFORM (1930s; manuscript)

    Composed at Mills College, Oakland, California.
    Score unlocated.
    Musical material later used for Suite for Chamber
     Orchestra (1939). See: W14.

W108. <u>MERELY A BEGINNING--STAGE FRIGHT</u> (1937; manuscript; 5 min.)

   Piano.
   Modern dance.
   Danced by Theatre Group in Boston.

W109. <u>A PASSING WORD</u> (1960; manuscript; 25 min.)   <u>See</u>: B55; C10; A2

   Flute/oboe/violoncello/piano.
   Ballet in six parts.
   Words by William B. Yeats.
   First lines: "Because I Long I am Not Complete"; "A
   Women's Beauty is Like a White Frail Bird"; "What
   Death"; "How Many Centuries Spent the Sedentary
   Soul"; "A Figure of Solitude"; "Bitter Reward of
   Many a Tragic Tomb."

   <u>Premiere</u>

   W109a.   1960 (Feb 27): Washington, D.C.; Roosevelt Audi-
            torium; Ethel Butler Dance Company; Ethel
            Butler, Meriam Rosen, Virginia Freeman, and
            Phillip Barretta, dancers; Esther Ballou,
            piano; Solomon Rosenthal, violoncello; Joseph
            Handlon, oboe; Gail Powell, flute. <u>See</u>: B51

W110. <u>POCOHANTAS GOES TO LONDON: A MUSICAL COMEDY</u> (1940s;
      manuscript; unfinished)

   Women's voices (parts only in manuscript).
   Book by Jerry Rand and Kurt Unkelbach.
   Lyrics by Jerry Rand and Connie Williams.
   Music by Esther Ballou (pen name: Connie Williams).
   Music and lyrics for four songs completed:
   "Prologue--Pocohantas Saved John Smith"; "Just as
   You Are'; "Home is a Feeling"; Virginia Laid Her
   Claim for Fame."
   First lines: "It Happened in Jamestown in Sixteen-
   O-Eight"; "I Love You Just as You Are"; "Home is
   Any Spot Where Love Abides"; "It Was Free, So
   They Claimed It."

W111. <u>POP GOES THE WEASEL</u> (1943; manuscript; incomplete)

   Piano (four hands).
   Modern dance.
   Choreography by José Limón.

W112. PRELUDE (1940s; manuscript; 4 min.)

>   Piano.
>   Modern dance.
>   Choreography by Eleanor Lauer.

W113. QUEST FOR THE DANCE (1960; manuscript; 3 min.)

>   Piano.
>   "For Linda Verrill."
>   Complete manuscript unlocated.

W114. TREE OF SINS (1960; manuscript; 11 min.)

>   Soprano/piano/percussion.
>   Modern dance.
>   Commissioned by Gertrude Lippincott.
>   Manuscript unlocated.
>   Cited in B71.

>   Premiere

>   W114a.   1961 (Apr 9): St. Paul, Minn.; Hamline University
>   Theater; Dance Repertory Group. See: B53

W115. TRIAL RUN (1969; manuscript; 6 min.)

>   1.(1 pic)/2.2.2/4.2.2.1/strings.
>   Documentary film.

W116. WAR LYRICS (1940; manuscript; 20 min.)

>   Trumpet/piano (four hands)/drums.
>   Ballet.
>   Three movements: "Blues Duet"; "Nurse Duet";
>   "Bacchanal."
>   Choreography by José Limón.
>   Composed at Mills College, Oakland, California.

Bibliography

"See" references refer to individual works and particular performances of those works as described in the "Works and Performances" section (e.g., See: W41c) and in the "Discography" (e.g., See: D1), and other citations in the "Bibliography" section.

B1.   "Alumni News." Juilliard Review (Winter 1957-58): 12.

        Cites a performance of the Trio for Violin, Violoncello, and Piano and Sonata for Piano at the composers Forum concert in New York. See: B35, B43, W41c, W72f

B2.   Ammer, Christine. Unsung: A History of Women in American Music (Westport, Conn.: Greenwood Press, 1980): 240, 242.

        Includes a brief biographical note on Ballou and mentions her Fellowship at the MacDowell Colony.

B3.   Anderson, Ruth. Contemporary American Composers: A Biographical Dictionary. 2nd ed. (Boston: G.K. Hall, 1982): 25.

        Includes a brief biographical note on Ballou with a selected list of compositions.

B4.   "AU Kreeger Music Building to be Dedicated Saturday." Northern Virginia Sun, October 27, 1966, p. 12.

        Includes biographical information on Ballou.

B5.   Backas, James. "Soprano Emma Porter Sings Best in
       Ravel." Washington Evening Star, December 13, 1966,
       p. A13.

       Review of a performance of "Wild Geese," "The
       Loiterer," and "Buffaloes" from Five Songs for
       Soprano by Emma Porter, soprano, and William
       Petterson, piano, on December 12, 1966 at the
       Phillips Gallery, Washington, D.C. "They were
       extremely well done and well received by the
       audience and seemed rather contrived and harmless to
       me." See: W90c

B6.   Ballou, Esther W. "Another Musical Myth." Music News
       (Newsletter of the Music Department, American Uni-
       versity), November 17, 1969, pp. 1-2.

       Discusses and dismisses the myth that the great com-
       posers somehow had great "magical powers." States,
       rather, that success at composing requires tedious
       work and long hours.

B7.   _____. "The Completion of the First Cycle of the New
       Theory Program at the American University, Theory
       VI: 'Late Romantic Music through Contemporary
       Music.'" Typescript, n.d., American University
       Archives.

       Overview of the program and the results of the final
       semester as taught by Ballou.

B8.   _____. "Creative Explorations of Musical Elements."
       Typescript, September 8, 1971, American University
       Archives.

       "The music student must learn from the beginning to
       conceive a musical idea, to notate it, however
       roughly, and then to perform it or to direct its
       performance. These are the basic requirements
       leading to a true understanding of music. This text
       provides the framework for the development of those
       requirements, starting from the most elementary
       level. A totally untutored music student can become
       a musician, providing he applies himself diligently
       to the materials contained herein, and he can enjoy
       doing it!" (p. iii.) This is a teacher's text which
       discusses rhythm-meter; pitch-melody; harmony-
       counterpoint in the context of lectures, suggested
       questions posed to the students, student exercises
       for use in-class, original student assignments,
       suggested examples provided in class by the teacher,
       and use of recordings. "Original written experi-
       ments in making music are outlined from the first
       chapter of this text. There are no rules given.

You must decide for yourself what is the right
answer for you. Class discussion is of the greatest
benefit to all participants. Teachers must learn to
admit that their formal image is a thing of the
past. Alert and creative thinking by teacher and
students is essential. Letting go of all prejudice
and opening your eyes to the material at hand will
be an exhilarating experience." (pp. iii-iv.)

B9.   . "Interpretation of Keyboard Music during the
Romantic Period." Typescript. Paper presented at
the Maryland State Music Teachers Association,
Peabody Conservatory of Music, Baltimore, Maryland,
June 25, 1963. American University Archives.

Interpretation is based on analysis, subliminal
judgement, and communication.

B10.   . "The Keyboard: What is an Artist?" National
Student Musician 2/3 (November 1964): 3.

Article was written October 16, 1964. A good performer is emotionally mature, musically versatile,
and places musicality above technical prowess. Includes photograph of Ballou.

B11.   . "Letter to the Editor." Washington Post, January 12, 1968, p. A16.

Written January 7, 1968, this editorial is a brief
touching eulogy on the death of Washington pianist
Harry McClure.

B12.   . "'Making Music': A New Approach to the Teaching of Theory." Typescript, Fall, 1968, American
University Archives.

Discusses the content and value of the theory program at American University.

B13.   . "A New Theory Program at American University."
Typescript, November 10, 1967, American University
Archives.

B14.   . Review of Harmonic Practice (New York:
Harcourt, Brace, and Co., 1951) by Roger Sessions.
Typescript, July-August, 1963, American University
Archives.

B15.   . Review of Twentieth Century Music (New York:
Pantheon Books, 1967) by Peter Yates in Music
Educators Journal 55/3 (November 1968): 124-25.

B16.   _____. "Theory with a Thrust." Music Educators
        Journal 55/1 (September 1968): 56-59.

        Discusses the experimental theory program at Ameri-
        can University; specifically focuses on elements and
        procedures for teaching basic harmony and theory,
        the first segment of the program; includes excerpts
        of student compositions.

B17.   _____. "Theory with a Thrust." Music Educators
        Journal 55/5 (January 1969): 55-57.

        Discusses the experimental theory program at Ameri-
        can University; specifically focuses on procedures
        for teaching twentieth century theory; includes ex-
        cerpt of a student composition.

B18.   "Ballou, Esther Williamson." Two Thousand Women of
        Achievement. 2nd ed. (London: Melrose Press, 1970):
        49.

        Includes a one-column biography, list of works, and
        a photograph of Ballou.

B19.   "Ballou, Esther Williamson." Who's Who in the East.
        14th ed. (Chicago: Marquis, 1973): 33.

        One-paragraph biography.

B20.   "Ballou, Esther Williamson." Who's Who of American
        Women. 7th ed. (Chicago: Marquis, 1971): 37.

        Brief biography. Also published in 1974-75 ed. (p.
        43) and 1975-76 ed. (p. 42).

B21.   Bennett, William. "Program at Phillips is Effective."
        Washington Evening Star, May 5, 1969, p. D7.

        Review of the May 4, 1969 premiere performance by
        Ervin Klinkon of Elegy for Solo Cello at the
        Phillips Gallery, Washington, D.C. "After intermis-
        sion came a work by local composer Esther Ballou
        which was composed to commemorate the death of
        Marian Davis. It is entitled Elegy for Solo Cello
        and was exactly that, an extremely sincere, well-
        written work that is highly effective in its evoca-
        tion of a reflective mood. The composer was on hand
        to receive well-earned applause. . . . The concert
        will be broadcast tonight on WAMU-FM." See: W81a

B22.   "Berlinski: Symphonic Visions." New Records 25/12
        (February 1958): 3.

The Composers Recordings, Inc. 115 recording which
includes Prelude and Allegro is cited but not re-
viewed. See: D1

B23.   Block, Adrienne Fried and Carol Neuls-Bates, eds.
       Women in American Music: A Bibliography of Music and
       Literature (Westport, Conn.: Greenwood Press, 1979):
       1, 149-50, 154, 156, 169-70, 183, 201, 207, 216.

       Lists sources for manuscripts, reviews, articles,
       and a recording.

B24.   Bostic, Ruth. "Notes on the Program; Meet the
       Artists." Stagebill 4/8 (April 1976): 17, 19, 38.

       Program notes for the April 9, 1976 performance of
       Nocturne for String Quartet at the Kennedy Center,
       Washington, D.C. performed by The Instrumental
       Ensemble, Jerzy Sapieyevski, conductor. Includes a
       brief biography and photograph of Ballou. See: W33a

B25.   Brockway, Thomas P. Bennington College: In the
       Beginning (Bennington, Vermont: Bennington College
       Press, 1981): 130, 156, 161, 165, 166.

       Mentions Ballou's contribution as a student to the
       early years of the college.

B26.   Bull, Storm. Index to Biographies of Contemporary
       Composers. 2 vols. (New York: Scarecrow Press,
       1964, 1974): 33 and 49, respectively.

       Volume 1 cites one biography; volume 2 cites ten
       reference works.

B27.   Campbell, Frank C. "Arts Club Hears Pianist McClure."
       Washington Evening Star, February 15, 1957, p. A28.

       Review of the February 14, 1957 performance by Harry
       McClure of the Sonata for Piano at the Arts Club,
       Washington, D.C. "The intent of Mrs. Ballou's Sona-
       ta is that of a major effort, with not a moment's
       relaxation of her very serious purpose. The texture
       favors leaness in skillfully wrought two and three-
       part counterpoint and widely spaced harmonies of a
       stark cast, even in the largest passages. The peak
       of the pieces comes in the fragile web of the second
       movement, and in the solemn statement of the chorale
       with its first few variations.
          On this second hearing I found more clarity and
       much ingenuity in the opening Allegro, but fragmen-
       tary and diffused materials still make it an elusive
       continuum, even for a Fantasia. Mrs. Ballou's re-
       markably consistent writing is marred only briefly

in the final variations, where some pedalled figura-
tions produce a momentary sonority that is a little
too lush for her canon of restraint and economy."
See: W72e

B28.   _____. "Fascinating Contrast Seen in CU Recital."
Washington Evening Star, May 13, 1957, p. B9.

Review of the May 12, 1957 performance by members of
Beta Phi Chapter of Sigma Alpha Iota, and Eta Theta
Chapter of Phi Mu Alpha of Suite for Winds. It was
described as "a little corker." "By means of witty
rhythms, pungent harmony, and masterly instrumenta-
tion she succeeded in writing three light-hearted
movements of grace and insouciance, in place of the
meaningless chapter [sic] often turned out for
groups of wind instruments." See: W39b

B29.   _____. "4 D.C. Composers Heard in Concert."
Washington Evening Star, May 12, 1958, p. B9.

Review of the May 11, 1958 performance by the
American University Quartet at American University
of the Divertimento. Mrs. Ballou is a composer of
"mature stature." "Mrs. Ballou's Divertimento is a
deftly fashioned piece, with arresting sonorities
created in the opening Allegro through lean widely-
spaced lines and in the final allegro through brash
parallelisms accompanying thematic materials. Song-
ful themes of the Siciliano are draped with grace
around the closely-woven harmonic fabric. I had
some impression yesterday of loose jointed formal
structure, but this could have resulted from a
performance that was hardly spic and span." See:
B46, W23a

B30.   _____. "Harry McClure Heard in Piano Recital."
Washington Evening Star, November 26, 1955, p. A12.

Review of the November 25, 1955 performance of the
Sonata for Piano at the Corcoran Gallery of Art,
Washington, D.C. "Esther Ballou's Sonata, opening
the second half of the programs [sic], was the impressive work of the evening for this reviewer.
Mrs. Ballou's writing has force and determination,
without being in the least merely straitforward
[sic]. The bare and angular proclamations of the
first section are as mystifying as are the deviously
twisting lines of a following andante. But the elu-
siveness is arresting, for the voice is confident,
the technique and invention perfectly assured. The
final Chorale Variations have the same authority,
with a logic that is much more intelligible on first
hearing." See: B42, W72b

B31.   Cleland, Daisy. "White House Changes Tune." <u>Washing-ton Evening Star</u>, September 7, 1963, p. A9.

      "The latter [<u>Capriccio</u>] was the last selection on the program and the composer who was in the audience was so moved by its success that she had tears in her eyes. 'I'm sorry,' she said, 'but I'm so moved and so excited.'" Includes a photograph of Ballou. <u>See</u>: W19a

B32.   Cohen, Aaron I. "Ballou, Esther Williamson." <u>International Encyclopedia of Women Composers</u> (New York: R.R. Bowker, 1981): 29-30.

      Includes a one-paragraph biography in which Ballou's place of death is cited incorrectly; includes a partial list of compositions and publishers.

B33.   Cohn, Arthur. Review of Composers Recordings, Inc. 115. <u>American Record Guide</u> 24/6 (February 1958): 298, 300.

      "It seems to me poor judgment to introduce Miss Ballou by choosing her <u>Prelude and Allegro</u>, a work of weak concession to the technique of multiple eclecticism. . . . Nor are the performances (even without recourse to the scores) more than passable." <u>See</u>: D1

B34.   "Comment Brightens AU Orchestra Concert." <u>Washington Evening Star</u>, May 20, 1960, p. A17.

      Review of the May 19, 1960 performance of the <u>Oboe Concertino</u> by the American University Orchestra, George Steiner, conducting, with Gerald Cotts, oboist at American University. "Miss Ballou's piece, written in 1953, and recently revised in honor of its first soloist, killed in the Navy Band's South American airplane crash, is a solid and moving piece that is well adapted to the characteristics [sic] technique of the oboe." Performed was likely <u>In Memoriam</u>. <u>See</u>: W9b

B35.   "Composers Forum Opens Concert Series." <u>New York Herald Tribune</u>, October 7, 1957.

      Review of the October 5, 1957 Composers Forum performance of the <u>Trio for Violin, Violoncello, and Piano</u> by Donald Portnoy, John Engberg, and Gene Akers, and the <u>Sonata for Piano</u> by Lionel Nowak at the McMillin Theater, Columbia University. "The andante of the trio ably combined a lyric and a tartar element. The finale was most persuasive in its exuberant close. The andante of the sonata, follow-

ing the spirited first section, dealt with its basic
theme too deliberately, but the music gained concen-
tration and color with the closing variations."
<u>See</u>: B1, B44, W41c, W72f

B36.   "Composers' World." <u>Musical America</u> 80 (July 1960):
        37.

        Cites the premiere performance of <u>In Memoriam</u> at the
        National Gallery of Art in Washington, D.C. on April
        3, 1960. <u>See</u>: W9a

B37.   "Concert Hall." <u>Bulletin. American Composers Alliance</u>
        2/4 (1952-53): 20.

        Cites the premiere performance of <u>Fantasia Brevis</u> at
        the Greenwood Music Camp, August 13 [1952]. <u>See</u>:
        W24a

B38.   "Concert Hall." <u>Bulletin. American Composers Alliance</u>
        3/1 (1953): 22.

        Cites a performance of <u>Prelude and Allegro</u> at the
        Phillips Gallery in Washington, D.C. on January 4,
        1953. Includes excerpts from a review in the <u>Wash-
        ington Post</u> for January 5. Cites the March 1, 1953
        performance of <u>Fantasia Brevis</u> I and II at the
        Kaufman Auditorium at Y.M.H.A. in New York. In-
        cludes a brief excerpt from a review in the <u>New York
        Herald Tribune</u> for March 2. <u>See</u>: W13b, W24b, W25a,
        B98, B158

B39.   "Concert Hall." <u>Bulletin. American Composers Alliance</u>
        3/4 (1953-54): 11.

        Cites dates and places for performances of <u>Suite for
        Violoncello and Piano</u> and <u>Sonata for Two Pianos</u>.
        Includes excerpts from reviews for the <u>Sonata for
        Two Pianos</u> in the <u>Washington Post</u> and <u>Washington
        Evening Star</u> for December 22, 1953. <u>See</u>: W38, W73a,
        B116, B200

B40.   "Concert Hall." <u>Bulletin. American Composers Alliance</u>
        4/1 (1954): 20.

        Cites excerpts from reviews of a performance of the
        <u>Oboe Concertino</u> at the Phillips Gallery, Wasington,
        D.C. in the <u>Washington Evening Star</u> and <u>Washington
        Post</u> for March 22, 1954. <u>See</u>: W12a, B199

B41.   "Concert Hall." <u>Bulletin. American Composers Alliance</u>
        5/2 (1955): 18.

Cites a performance of the <u>Sonata for Piano</u>, the composer performing, at the Phillips Gallery, Washington, D.C. on March 7, 1955. Also includes excerpts from newspaper reviews. <u>See</u>: W72a, B106, B144

B42.   "Concert Hall." <u>Bulletin</u>. <u>American Composers Alliance</u> 5/3 (1956): 16.

Cites the review in the <u>Washington Evening Star</u>, November 26, 1955 of the <u>Sonata for Piano</u> performed by Harry McClure at the Corcoran Gallery, Washington, D.C. on November 25, 1955. <u>See</u>: W72b, B30

B43.   "Concert Hall." <u>Bulletin</u>. <u>American Composers Alliance</u> 6/1 (1956): 14.

Cites performances and excerpts for reviews of <u>Sonata for Piano</u>, Lionel Nowak performing at the Bennington Composers Conference on August 12, 1956; and <u>Trio for Violin, Violoncello, and Piano</u> performed at the Phillips Gallery, Washington, D.C. on March 19, 1956. <u>See</u>: W72c, W73, W41a, B1, B101

B44.   "Concert Hall." <u>Bulletin</u>. <u>American Composers Alliance</u> 7/2 (1958): 23.

Cites performances of the <u>Trio for Violin, Violoncello, and Piano</u> by Max Pollikoff, violin, George Finkel, violoncello, and Esther Ballou, piano, at the Bennington Composers' Conference in Bennington, Vermont on August 21, 1957, and by Donald Portnoy, violin, John Engberg, violoncello, and Gene Akers, piano at the Composers' Forum at Columbia University on October 5, 1957. On the latter program was a performance by Lionel Nowak of the <u>Sonata for Piano</u>. Reviews are cited from the <u>New York Herald Tribune</u> and the <u>New York Times</u>. <u>See</u>: W41b, W41c, W72f, B35, B67

B45.   "Concert Hall." <u>Bulletin</u>. <u>American Composers Alliance</u> 7/4 (1958): 22.

Cites a performance of the <u>Trio for Violin, Violoncello, and Piano</u> on February 23, 1958 in Washington, D.C. <u>See</u>: W41

B46.   "Concert Hall." <u>Bulletin</u>. <u>American Composers Alliance</u> 8/1 (1958): 21.

Cites performances and reviews of <u>Suite for Winds</u> by the U.S. Air Force Symphonette, Colonel George S. Howard, conducting, at the Corcoran Gallery , Washington, D.C. on March 23, 1958; <u>Divertimento</u> per-

formed at the Phillips Gallery on May 11, 1958 with
an excerpt from a review in the <u>Washington Evening
Star</u> by Frank G. Campbell; and <u>Beguine</u> at the Cosmos
Club Assembly Hall of the Friday Morning Music Club,
Washington, D.C. on April 18, 1958 by Alice and
Arthur Nagle, duo-pianists and again in the music
room of Mrs. Anne Archbold of Washington, D.C. on
April 27, 1958. <u>See</u>: W39c, W23a, W48a, W48b, B29,
respectively

B47.   "Concert Hall." <u>Bulletin</u>. <u>American Composers Alliance</u>
8/2 (1959): 21.

Cites reviews, times, and places for several works
by Ballou.

B48.   "Concert Hall." <u>Bulletin</u>. <u>American Composers Alliance</u>
8/3 (1959): 20.

Cites a performance of <u>Prelude and Allegro</u> at Cooper
Union, Howard Shanet, conducting, in New York on
January 16, 1959. <u>See</u>: W13d

B49.   "Concert Hall." <u>Bulletin</u>. <u>American Composers Alliance</u>
9/1 (1959): 19.

Cites the premiere performance of <u>Sonata for Two
Pianos No. 2</u> by Margaret Ann McConnell and Carolyn
Osborne at the Alpha Iota National Convention in San
Francisco, California on August 8, 1959. <u>See</u>: W74a

B50.   "Concert Hall." <u>Bulletin</u>. <u>American Composers Alliance</u>
9/2 (1960): 18.

Cites the following performances: <u>Sonata for Two
Pianos</u> by Alice and Arthur Eaton (actually Nagle?),
duo-pianists at Iowa State Teachers College, Cedar
Falls Iowa, on October 13, 1959; <u>Prelude and Allegro</u>
by Evelyn Swarthout, piano and Emerson Meyers, conductor (ensemble not cited) at the Powell Auditorium, Friday Morning Morning Music Club, Washington,
D.C. on December 4, 1959; <u>A Babe is Born</u> premiered
by the American University Chorus, Gordon H. Smith,
conductor, at Clendenen Hall, American University,
Washington, D.C. <u>See</u>: W74b, W13c, W82a, respectively

B51.   "Concert Hall." <u>Bulletin</u>. <u>American Composers Alliance</u>
9/3 (1960): 26.

Cites dates and places for performances of three
works: <u>A Passing Word</u> (premiere) by Ethel Butler,
Meriam Rosen, Virginia Freeman, and Phillip
Barretta, dancers, Esther Ballou, piano, Solomon

Rosenthal, cello, Joseph Handlon, oboe, and Gail
Powell, flute, at Roosevelt Auditorium, Washington,
D.C. on February 27, 1960; Sonata for Two Pianos No.
2 by Alice and Arthur Nagle, duo-pianists at Catholic University of America on March 20, 1960; and
Variations, Scherzo and Fugue for piano (premiere)
by Evelyn Swarthout at the Friday Morning Music Club
on March 26, 1960. See: W109a, W74c, W80a, respectively

B52.   "Concert Hall." Bulletin. American Composers Alliance
       9/4 (1961): 19.

       Cites performances and excerpts from reviews of the
       Washington Post and Washington Evening Star for In
       Memoriam and Oboe Concertino. See: W9, W12

B53.   "Concert Hall." Bulletin. American Composers Alliance
       10/3 (1962): 34.

       Cites performance of Tree of Sins by the Dance Rep-
       ertory Group at Hamline University Theater on April
       9, 1961. See: W114a

B54.   "Concert Hall." Bulletin. American Composers Alliance
       11/2-4 (1963): 30.

       Cites dates and places for performances of Beguine
       and Rondino. See: W2, W71

B55.   "Concert Hall." Bulletin. American Composers Alliance
       12/1 (1964): 16.

       Cites the following works and performances: The
       Beatitudes, Metropolitan Memorial Methodist Church,
       Washington, D.C., November 17, 1962; Capriccio, the
       White House, September 6, 1963, and Convention of
       the Maryland Music Teachers Association, November 3,
       1963; Passacaglia and Toccata National Cathedral,
       October 6, 1963; A Passing Word, Western High
       School, Washington, D.C., January 18, 1964; Varia-
       tions, Scherzo and Fugue on a Theme by Lou Harrison,
       Southern Connecticut State College, May 9, 1963,
       College of William and Mary, Williamsburg, Virginia,
       May 19, 1963, Brooklyn Museum, June 12, 1963, Con-
       vention of Maryland Music Teachers Association, No-
       vember 5, 1963, First Unitarian Church, Berkeley,
       California, September 28, 1963; Street Scenes,
       Corcoran Gallery of Art, Washington, D.C., January
       1964. See: W84a, W19a, W64b, B55, W109, W80d, W98,
       respectively

B56.   "Concert Hall." Bulletin. American Composers Alliance
       13/1 (1965): 24.

Cites the following works and performances: <u>Capriccio</u>, <u>Five Songs</u> (<u>Early American Portrait</u>) and <u>Sonata for Piano</u> (1954) at the John Wesley Powell Auditorium, Friday Morning Music Club, April 24, 1964; <u>Concerto for Solo Guitar and Chamber Orchestra</u>, American University, May 22, 1964; <u>Variations, Scherzo and Fugue on a Theme by Lou Harrison</u>, San Diego State University, Selma Epstein, piano, Brooklyn Museum, June 23, 1964, Selma Epstein, piano, American University, July 27, 1964, Evelyn Swarthout, piano, and Phillips Academy, Andover, Massachusetts, August 2, 1964, Evelyn Swarthout, piano. <u>See</u>: W19c, W90a, W72i, W7a, W80e, W80f

B57.   "Concert Hall." <u>Washington Calendar Magazine</u> (1978, no. 7): 18.

Notice of a forthcoming performance of an Esther Ballou memorial concert on April 10, 1978 at American University. <u>See</u>: W19g, W21b, W26e, W36f, W73f

B58.   "Concert Music." <u>BMI: The Many Worlds of Music</u> (April 1971): 14.

Notes that Esther Ballou is co-director of the composers Residency Program of the Wolf Trap American University Academy for the Performing Arts.

B59.   "Concert Music: Festivals." <u>About BMI Music and Writers</u> (October 1964): 19.

Cites a performance of <u>Variations, Scherzo and Fugue</u> at the Matthay Piano Festival at the Phillips Academy, Andover, Massachusetts, July 29-August 6, 1964. Includes a photograph of Ballou. <u>See</u>: W80f, B56

B60.   Cordovana, Michael. "New Work Presented in Duet Piano Recital." <u>Washington Post</u>, April 24, 1963.

Review of the April 23, 1963 piano recital by Esther Ballou and Evelyn Swarthout at Clendenen Hall, American University. "The program presented was difficult and contained representative works from every period beginning with the Baroque. The pianists met this stylistic challenge with knowledgeable skill and authority."

B61.   Crowder, Charles. "D.C. Composer has Perfect Setting." <u>Washington Post</u>, March 22, 1965, p. B8.

A review of the following performances at the Unitarian Church in Arlington, Virginia: <u>In Memoriam</u> by members of the National Gallery Orchestra, Richard Bales, conductor, with Beth Sears, oboist; <u>Early</u>

<u>American Portrait</u> by Katherine Hansel, soprano, and
members of the orchestra; <u>Concerto for Solo Guitar
and Chamber Orchestra</u> by Robert Luse, guitarist,
and members of the orchestra; and <u>Prelude and Allegro for String Orchestra and Piano</u> by Esther Ballou,
piano, and members of the orchestra. "It was the
first occasion I have had to hear an entire concert
of her works, and the over-all impression was strong
and immensely moving.

Perhaps the strongest thought is that Mrs. Ballou
has found the means to transfer the most subtle of
her reactions into sound. And in a day when composers have taken to obscuring personal emotions with-
in tight, intellectual techniques it is refreshing
to hear one speak with such courageous candor.

This aspect of her music is couched in a craft
that works for projection rather than hiding it.
Yet craft never interrupts a musical flow that is
free, rather improvisational in character. Her
melodic, harmonic and contrapuntal thinking is inventive and imaginative, adapting to the mood being
expressed.

Listening to Mrs. Ballou's music is a pleasure,
not an intellectual exercise, and when there are
fine performing artists involved, the pleasure is
heightened. The afternoon began with a piece called
"In Memoriam" dedicated to the late William Carl
Fels, president of Bennington College until 1964.
The easy and tender flow of the piece came to the
ears with the sight of the sunlit oaks and pines
overhead. It was an artistic experience long to be
remembered.

Richard Bales conducted members of the National
Gallery Orchestra, with Beth Sears as oboe soloist.
The concept and warm attachment of the performance
left the full house with a moment or two of silence
before the ovation broke forth.

Soprano Katherine Hansel sang the first public
performance of five songs called "Early American
Portrait," with Mrs. Ballou at the piano. In an
afternoon filled with moments of beauty, special
mention should be made of Mrs. Hansel's superb way
with these songs. They are fascinating, a tour de
force in combination of melody, text and piano comments on the text.

The 1964 Guitar Concerto was admirably played by
Robert Luse one of the finest of the young set of
guitarists in town. Another performance with more
clearly defined balances will be welcome any time.

Mrs. Ballou joined Bales and the orchestra to
close the concert with the 1949 "Prelude and Allegro." Their performance and those that came before
brought Mrs. Ballou and her music an ovation." <u>See</u>:
W9c, W8a, W7a, W13e, respectively

B62.   _____. "Esther Ballou's '5-4-3': New Work Heard at
        Kindler Concert." Washington Post, June 14, 1966,
        p. B7.

        A review of the June 12, 1966 performance by Rilla
        Mervine, mezzo-contralto, Richard Parnas, viola, and
        Sylvia Meyer, Harp, of 5-4-3 at the Textile Museum
        in Washington, D.C. "Mrs. Ballou has done some very
        special reacting to this poetry, for as in reading
        this poet's work, with the space-time element of
        gathering peripheral thoughts while reading the
        carefully spaced lines of uncapitalized words, she
        has translated her own personal reactions into
        sounds that capture fleeting introspections, some-
        times strong, sometimes tender, always to the point
        and mirroring the growing complexities of the
        poet's thoughts.
          Each of the five songs carried a distinct and mov-
        ing message--the kind of music that captures your
        imagination and holds it." This review was first
        published in the Washington Post, June 13, 1966,
        under the title "New Work by Esther W. Ballou High-
        lights Foundation's Concert." See: W26a

B63.   Daniel, Oliver. "The New Festival." Bulletin. Ameri-
        can Composers Alliance 5/1 (1955): 3-4.

        Discusses Ballou's approach to composition. Mrs.
        Ballou feels that she needs a deadline toward which
        to compose ". . . and a very definite one! If no
        such deadline exists, I can think of semmingly
        countless ways to postpone working. This has been a
        pattern during all my composing life. Creating
        one's own deadline doesn't seem to work. Convincing
        one's own subconscious of the urgency for a complet-
        ed work, without some definite performance in mind,
        is a problem I haven't been able to solve." In-
        cludes excerpts from newspaper reviews.

B64.   "Deaths." Mills Quarterly 56/1 (August 1973): 62.

        Obituary. States Ballou "was regarded as one of the
        leading composers in this country and as an out-
        standing pianist."

B65.   "Dinner, Concert Plans Set for Annual Program." Amer-
        ican University Eagle, December 9, 1959, p. 1.

        Cites the premiere performance of A Babe is Born to
        take place on December 17, 1959 at Clendenen Hall,
        American University by the AU Chorus, Gordon H.
        Smith, conductor. See: W82a

B66.   Donaldson, Michael. "Notes on the Program." <u>Stage-</u>
        <u>bill</u> 4/6 (February 1976): 30A, 31B-32A.

        Program notes for the February 23, 1976 performance
        of <u>Sonata for Two Pianos No. 2</u> by Alice and Arthur
        Nagle, duo-pianists, at the Kennedy Center, Washing-
        ton, D.C. The program was titled "The Bicentennial
        Parade of American Music." <u>See</u>: W74d

B67.   Downes, Edward. "Season Opens for Composers Forum."
        <u>New York Times</u>, October 7, 1957, p. 22.

        Review of the October 5, 1957 performance of the
        <u>Trio</u> by Donald Portnoy, violin, John Engberg,
        violoncello, and Gene Akers, piano, and the <u>Sonata</u>
        <u>for Piano</u> by Lionel Nowak at the Composers Forum at
        Columbia University. "Mrs. Ballou was represented
        by two fluent works, a piano sonata written in 1954
        and a Trio for violin, 'cello and piano written in
        1955. Both used a modified twelve-tone technique in
        their slow movements, but without destroying a
        strong basic impression of tonality.
          Despite the apparent ease with which Mrs. Ballou
        handled traditional forms, such as sonata-allegro
        and rondo, the musical material did not seem to this
        listener very imaginatively or interestingly devel-
        oped." <u>See</u>: W41c

B68.   "DPA Receives Bequest of Piano, Music Library." <u>Amer-</u>
        <u>ican University Reporter</u> 13/20 (February 2, 1982): 3

        One-column announcement of bequest of Ballou's li-
        brary of music material to American University.

B69.   <u>Edwin A. Fleisher Collection of Orchestral Music in</u>
        <u>the Free Library of Philadelphia: A Cumulative</u>
        <u>Catalog, 1929-1977</u> (Boston: G.K. Hall, 1979): 56.

        Lists three compositions held in the Free Library:
        <u>Concerto for Piano</u> (1965), <u>Oboe Concertino</u>, and <u>Pre-</u>
        <u>lude and Allegro</u>. <u>See</u>: W5, W12, W13

B70.   "Elmira Girl to Play Own Music Composition over New
        York Radio Station." <u>Elmira Advertiser</u>, November 6,
        1936.

        A two-column notice of Ballou's <u>Impertinence for</u>
        <u>Clarinet and Piano</u> to be performed by the composer
        and Robert McBride, clarinetist, over radio station
        WABC. Includes a photograph and biographical infor-
        mation on Ballou. <u>See</u>: 28a

B71.   "Esther Ballou." Brochure (New York: Broadcast Music,
        Inc., 1968).

Includes biographical information, excerpts from reviews, a list of works, and a photograph of Ballou.

B72.   "Esther Ballou, 57, Dies; Pianist and Composer."
        Washington Evening Star, March 14, 1973, p. B6.

        Two-column obituary.

B73.   "Esther W. Ballou." Composers of the America 9
        (1963): 13-18.

        Includes a catalog of Ballou's works, including
        dates and places of performances. Also included is
        a photograph of Ballou and an excerpt of the Capric-
        cio for Violin and Piano. See: W19

B74.   "Esther Williamson Ballou Fund Sponsors NRT Music
        Tour." Bennington College Quadrille 12/1 (Spring
        1978): 14.

        Discusses a special music fund in honor of Ballou in
        the Music Division at the college and a number of
        performances sponsored through the fund.

B75.   "Esther Williamson Ballou." Mills Quarterly (February
        1965): 28.

        A two-column notice of Ballou receiving an honorary
        doctorate from Hood College. 'Includes biographical
        information and a photograph of Ballou.

B76.   "Esther Williamson Ballou: Sonata for Two Pianos
        (1949)," record jacket notes (New York: Composers
        Recordings, Inc. SD 472, 1982).

        "Sonata for Two Pianos begins in the second piano
        with a four-note ostinato figure cutting across bar
        lines; the first pianist counters with a lengthy
        thematic statement in a contrasting rhythm. The
        second movement, like the first, makes its musical
        points with long sweeping phrases, but this time
        more slowly, and the atmosphere is altogether calmer
        and more deliberate. It ends in a long crescendo
        trill that leads immediately into the third move-
        ment, a sparkling 'Allegro vivace.' There are de-
        ceptively quiet interludes, the last of these again
        introduced by a long trill. The sonata then builds
        up to a brilliant 'fortississimo' climax, with a
        a dissonant unresolved chord flung defiantly five
        times into the air." See: D2

B77.   "Evelyn Swarthout to Appear in Recital." Daily News
        of the Virgin Islands, March 28, 1972.

Notice of a forthcoming performance of the <u>Varia-</u>
<u>tions, Scherzo, and Fugue on a Theme by Lou Harrison</u>
on April 3, 1972. <u>See</u>: W80i

B78. Evett, Robert. "Performance for Peace is Suitably
      Non-Grim." <u>Washington Evening Star</u>, September 28,
      1970, p. C7.

      Review of the September 27, 1970 performance of <u>Hear</u>
      <u>Us!</u> by the American University Singers, Vito Mason,
      conducting, at Metropolitan Memorial Methodist
      Church, Washington, D.C. "Esther Ballou's piece
      'Hear Us,' for chorus and organ, is a highly idio-
      matic and forceful setting of the Lord's Prayer em-
      bellished with fragments of other religious state-
      ments. The performance did not seem especially pol-
      ished, but it was serviceable." <u>See</u>: W85d

B79. Famera, Karen McNerney. <u>Catalog of the American Music</u>
      <u>Center Library. Volume 2: Chamber Music</u> (New York:
      American Music Center, 1978): 112.

      Cites <u>5-4-3</u>, its instrumentation, publisher, and du-
      ration. <u>See</u>: W26

B80. "First Composer's Cabin at Wolf Trap: Piano Gift of
      Washington Alumnae Chapter, SAI." <u>Pan Pipes of Sig-</u>
      <u>ma Alpha Iota</u> 66/2 (January 1974).

      In the Composer's Cabin at the Wolf Trap Farm Park
      "Filene Center" for the Performing Arts in McLean,
      Virginia is a piano with the following inscription:
      "GIFT of the WASHINGTON ALUMNAE CHAPTER of SIGMA
      ALPHA IOTA In memory of ESTHER BALLOU and DELVA
      DILLAWAY 1973."

B81. Frasier, Jane. <u>Women Composers: A Discography</u> (De-
      troit: Information Coordinators, 1983): 10.

      Cites recording of <u>Prelude and Allegro</u> released by
      Composers Recordings, Inc. 115. <u>See</u>: D1

B82. Frome, Faith. "Spotlight--A Composer: She's Teaching
      Kids How to HEAR Music." <u>Montgomery County Senti-</u>
      <u>nel</u>, July 16, 1964, p. B7.

      A lengthy biography of Ballou, and describes her
      musical aesthetics. "I realize now how fortunate I
      was in the beginning. The feeling for music was not
      only encouraged in the home, but my teacher too com-
      municated a respect and love for its beauty. I be-
      lieve that this communication is invaluable to a
      child." Includes a photograph of Ballou.

B83.   Gerber, Leslie. Review of Composers Recordings, Inc.
        472. Fanfare 6/5 (May/June 1983): 272-73.

        Review of Sonata for Two Pianos (1949). Esther
        Williamson Ballou (1915-1973) is certainly the most
        obscure composer on this disc. . . . The music
        seems to meander without much point through its
        first two movements, but the finale builds up con-
        siderable motor energy with some good contrasts. It
        is well worth waiting for. . . . The Grunschlags
        . . . give a fine account of themselves throughout
        this recital. They play with fine tone. . . and
        plenty of impulse, and they make whatever points the
        music has to offer." See: D2

B84.   "Glimpses of New Music by American Composers." Pan
        Pipes of Sigma Alpha Iota 56/2 (January 1964): 13.

        Notice of premiere of Capriccio at the White House.
        See: W19a

B85.   Greene, Frank. Composers on Record (Metuchen, N.J.:
        Scarecrow Press, 1985): 30.

        Includes five references to writings on Ballou.

B86.   Grueninger, Walter F. "Recorded Music in Review."
        Consumer's Research Magazine 66/10 (October 1983):
        43.

        Review of Sonata for Two Pianos (1949) on Composers
        Recordings, Inc. 472. "No masterpieces here but di-
        versity of styles in the four compositions provides
        interest. . . . The Grunschlags play ably,
        straightforwardly." See: D2

B87.   Haskins, John. "Concert Features Local Artists."
        Washington Post, May 12, 1958, p. B14.

        Review of the May 11, 1958 performance by American
        University String Quartet of Divertimento at the
        Phillips Gallery. "A recent Divertimento for quar-
        tet by Ballou began the proceedings with an angular
        Allegro agitato, an affecting Siciliano, and a jumpy
        little Allegro in scherzo style. The composer
        shared in the applause the work drew from a medium-
        sized audience." See: W23a

B88.   _____. "Contemporary Works Heard." Washington Eve-
        ning Star, April 23, 1965, p. B7.

        Review of the April 22, 1965 performance by Nancy
        Ellsworth, violin, and Esther Ballou, piano, of the

<u>Capriccio for Violin and Piano</u> at American
University. "The Ballou Capriccio, played by Nancy
Ellsworth with the composer at the piano, was con-
ventional in form, modern in idiom and lyrical in
feeling, neatly crafted and neatly played." <u>See</u>:
W19d

B89.   _____. "Piano Duetists Give Program." <u>Washington
Evening Star</u>, April 24, 1963, p. E15.

Review of a recital by duo-pianists Esther Ballou
and Evelyn Swarthout on April 23, 1963 at American
University. Ballou's arrangement of "Contrapunctus
V and IX" from Bach's <u>Art of the Fugue</u> was performed
as was works by Bartók, Mozart, Schubert,
Stravinsky, Debussy, and Heiden. <u>See</u>: W47a

B90.   Heintze, James R. "Ballou Collection." <u>American
University Report</u> (November/December 1973): 16.

Notice of a special collection consisting of
Ballou's publications, scores, and manuscripts to be
established at American University.

B91.   _____. "Ballou, Esther (Williamson)." <u>New Grove
Dictionary of Music and Musicians</u>, ed. by Stanley
Sadie (London: Macmillan, 1980) 2: 97.

One-column biography and a selective list of works.

B92.   _____. "In Memory of Esther Williamson Ballou."
<u>Notes</u> 30/1 (September 1973): 39.

Notice of the establishment at American University
of the Esther Ballou Memorial Collection consisting
of her publications, scores, and documents related
to her life.

B93.   Hinson, Maurice. <u>Guide to the Pianist's Repertoire</u>
(Bloomington: Indiana University Press, 1973): 51.

Annotated entries for <u>Sonata for Piano</u> (1954) and
<u>Variations, Scherzo and Fugue on a Theme by Lou
Harrison</u>. <u>See</u>: W72, W80

B94.   _____. <u>Music for More than One Piano: An Annotated
Guide</u> (Bloomington: Indiana University Press, 1983):
10.

Includes an entry for the <u>Beguine</u> and <u>Sonata for Two
Pianos</u>. <u>See</u>: W48, W73

B95.   _____. <u>Music for Piano and Orchestra: An Annotated
Guide</u> (Bloomington, Indiana University Press): 20.

Includes entries for the <u>Concerto for Piano</u> (1965)
and <u>Prelude and Allegro</u>. <u>See</u>: W5, W13

B96.   Hixon, Don L. and Don Hennessee. <u>Women in Music: A
Biobibliography</u> (Metuchen, N.J.: Scarecrow Press,
1975): 17.

Cites two biographical sources.

B97.   Hume, Paul. "American Music at Catholic U." <u>Washing-
ton Post</u>, November 17, 1958, p. B16.

Review of the November 16, 1958 performance by members of Sigma Alpha Iota and Phi Mu Alpha of the <u>Di-
vertimento</u> at Catholic University of America, Washington, D.C. "The Ballou Divertimento is sure,
bright with melodic and rhythmic ideas that remain
fresh, and the manipulation of a hand that never
slips." <u>See</u>: W23b

B98.   _____. "Ballou Work Given Twice at Phillips."
<u>Washington Post</u>, January 5, 1953, p. 13.

Review of the January 4, 1953 performance by Esther
Ballou, piano, and the Olefsky Chamber Orchestra,
Paul Olevsky, conductor, of <u>Prelude and Allegro</u>. ".
. . A filled gallery heard a program which included
the first performance of an excellent piece by
Esther Williamson Ballou entitled Prelude and Allegro. Written in 1951, the music was played second
and fourth on the program. This idea of giving two
hearings to a new work is one many small and large
organizations might well consider in order to make
easier the matter of understanding and assessing new
works. . . . The Ballou work is extremely well
written for strings and piano. It was considerably
fortified by the singularly expert pianism of the
composer herself. The prelude is a contrast between contrapuntal writing for the strings and a
chorale-like figure in the piano. Here and in the
genuinely flashing allegro, were more than once re-
minded of the style of Walter Piston in his rather
similar Prelude and Allegro for strings and organ."
<u>See</u>: W13b, B38

B99.   _____. "Concerts for Peace." <u>Washington Post</u>, September 21, 1970, p. B9.

Notice of a forthcoming concert to take place at
Metropolitan Memorial Methodist Church on September
27, 1970 to bring attention to the Vietnam War.
Included on the program will be a work by Esther
Ballou. <u>See</u>: W85d, B78, B121

B100.   _____. "Elmira Bier." <u>Washington Post</u>, February 22,
         1976, pp. G1, G3.

         Cites Esther Ballou as one of a number of Washing-
         ton, D.C. composers whose music was regularly per-
         formed at the Phillips Gallery. Elmira Bier was
         associated with the Gallery for some forty-nine
         years and scheduled many of the concerts there.

B101.   _____. "Fine Music Presented at Phillips."
         <u>Washington Post</u>, March 20, 1956, p. 35.

         Review of the March 19, 1956 performance of the <u>Trio</u>
         by Esther Ballou, piano, James Barber, violin, and
         John Engberg, violoncello. "Esther Williamson
         Ballou's new piano trio had a first hearing. . . .
         This is a work that ought to be taken up by any
         piano trio in search of something new that will at
         once make its way with audiences. There is an un-
         usual factor in this composer who has a fine gift
         for writing well and at the same time in a way that
         attracts musicians and amateurs.
         The opening movement goes with great spirit,
         marked by complete understanding of the two stringed
         instruments, and with solid piano writing. The
         piano is spaced so that the quieter strings can be
         heard either above it, or by themselves.
         The slow movement opens in highly persuasive man-
         ner, and then, it seemed at first hearing, lapsed a
         bit into something less original. This may disap-
         pear on second hearing. In any case, nothing must
         change the final pages of the movement which build,
         in receding levels of sound, to an impressive close.
         The finale is an allegro of dash, compounded of
         themes that take intriguing turns." <u>See</u>: W41a,
         B43

B102.   _____. "Ivan Romanenko's Recital Impressive." <u>Wash-
         ington Post</u>, December 21, 1966, p. B9.

         Review of the performance of <u>Capriccio for Violin
         and Piano</u> by Ivan Romanenko, violin, and Joan
         Singer, piano, on December 19, 1966 at the Phillips
         Gallery, Washington, D.C. "The Ballou Capriccio is
         a fanciful business, free in form, though it turns
         fugal before it is over. In spite of its sense of
         freedom, it has some very rigid requirements that
         proved difficult for the violin. Only in the clos-
         ing pages did the performance rise to the breadth of
         the writing." <u>See</u>: W19e

B103.   _____. "Jane White Gives Warmth to Fine Songs."
         <u>Washington Post</u>, November 22, 1966, p. D10.

Review of the November 21, 1966 performance by Jane
White, soprano, and Sara Klinkon, piano, at the
Phillips Gallery, Washington, D.C., of four of <u>Five
Songs for Soprano</u>. "An unusual set of four songs
brought the recital to a close in Esther Ballou's
music for poems from 'American Frontier' by
Elisabeth Peck. Simple but moving poems about life
in this country in the 19th century, these draw on
every day matters from Kentucky, Iowa, and North
Carolina. Mrs. Ballou has found for three of them
apposite music of distinct flavor. Only in the
final, 'Democracy,' did the music seem to interfere
with the natural flow and meaning of the words,
though the singer brought the spirit of the poem
right to the front." <u>See</u>: W90b

B104. _____. "Musician Esther Williamson Ballou; Composer,
Pianist; Taught at CU, AU." <u>Washington Post</u>, March
14, 1973, p. C6.

Three-column obituary. Includes 1952 photograph.
"A former student [of Ballou] commented yesterday
that even those in her classes who did not like the
routine of music theory were enthusiastic about her
teaching. The lucidity of thought that marked her
teaching was also a constant factor in her music."

B105. _____. "National Gallery Concert a Significant Land-
mark." <u>Washington Post</u>, June 8, 1965, p. B6.

Review of the June 6, 1965 performance by the National Gallery of Art Orchestra, Richard Bales, conductor, with Charles Crowder, piano, of the <u>Concerto
for Piano</u>. "Cast in more than three movements, like
concertos of the other 'B'composers Brahms and
Busoni, the new work is in the big, romantic manner.
Mrs. Ballou, herself a pianist of substantial abilities, writes with the knowledge of an expert. The
first movement, marked 'maestoso-allegro moderato,'
moved largely in a slow, rather ponderous manner
with more that a little bombast.
  With the scherzo, which draws heavily upon celes-
ta, xylophone, and other assorted percussion, and
very light, rapid piano writing, things moved more
brightly. It is the slow movement, however, that is
the crown of the work, and a beautifully constructed
movement it is. In arch form, it moves from an elo-
quent violin solo through several solo passages for
the piano, into passages of quite exalted expres-
siveness.
  The finale returns again to the Lisztian school of
passage work, but with more interest than the opening." <u>See</u>: W5a

B106.   _____. "Phillips Gallery Concert by Composers' Chapter." <u>Washington Post</u>, March 8, 1955, p. 14.

Review of the March 7, 1955 performance by Esther Ballou of her <u>Sonata for Piano</u> (1954) at the Phillips Gallery, Washington, D.C. "First performance went to a striking Sonata by Mrs. Ballou, who serves as her own pianist, and most handsomely so. Her music, unlike some contemporary writing for piano, remembers the singing qualities of the instrument as well as some of its finest sonorities. But it is a classic work built along lines that recall the eighteenth century, with rolling ornaments and linear development that give a great sense of power. The slow movement is a profoundly felt, and amazingly simply devised melodic sequence. It has an inevitability about it and a kind of utter calm that reminds us of the slow movement of the Beethoven Opus 135." <u>See</u>: W72a, B41

B107.   _____. "Pianist Plays to Jammed Gallery." <u>Washington Post</u>, May 8, 1961, p. A26.

Review of the May 7, 1961 performance by the composer at the Phillips Gallery, Washington, D.C. The concert included works by Bach, Scarlatti, Chopin, Schumann, and Ellis Kohs. "It was interesting, too, to note with what ease Mrs. Ballou dispatched every facet of the Kohs piece, handling its musical problems with great authority, and its pianistic challenge with ease."

B108.   _____. "A Premiere Concert, in Memoriam." <u>Washington Post</u>, January 15, 1978, p. M12.

Discusses the 25th anniversary of the Kindler Foundation concerts, in which each year is presented the premiere of a compositions "in the name of Hans Kindler, the founder and first conductor of the National Symphony Orchestra." Of the twenty-four previously commissioned works, Ballou's <u>5-4-3</u> is cited as among "a few that proved memorable." <u>See</u>: W26

B109.   _____. "Quintet Plays Seldom-Heard Music." <u>Washington Post</u>, May 19, 1966, p. C6.

Review of a recital by the National Capital Wind Quintet with Esther Ballou as guest pianist on May 18, 1966 at American University. Regarding Ballou's playing, Hume comments that she and James London, horn player, "played with immense gusto and tonal beauty. . . ." Works by Beethoven, Roussel, and Verne Reynolds were performed.

B110.   _____.   Review of Piano Recital at Phillips Gallery.
         <u>Washington Post</u>, November 3, 1958, p. B6.

         One-paragraph review of a performance of the <u>Sonata</u>
         <u>for Piano</u> on November 2, 1958 by Helen McGraw at the
         Phillips Gallery, Washington, D.C. <u>See</u>: W72g

B111.   _____.   "Rich Program Sung by Rilla Mervine at
         Phillips Gallery." <u>Washington Post</u>, October 19,
         1966, p. C7.

         Review of a performance by Rilla Mervine, mezzo-
         contralto, Richard Parnas, viola, and Faith Carman,
         harp, of <u>5-4-3</u> on October 17, 1966. "The meanings,
         and more, the often susurrant Cummings words find
         such matching moods in the music that they seem al-
         most to have been designed for the sound of the sib-
         ilant harp, though that instrument is at times used
         as a drum and at other times with a papery quality.
         Each instrument has a distinctive profile in the
         songs, with the viola coming, at the last, to a per-
         fect unison with the voice. These are a distin-
         guished achievement." The review was first pub-
         lished in the late edition of the <u>Washington Post</u>,
         October 18, 1966, under the title "Rilla Mervine in
         Song Recital." <u>See</u>: W26b

B112.   _____.   "Robert Parris Pleases at the Harpsichord."
         <u>Washington Post</u>, January 3, 1962, p. C7.

         Review of <u>Rondino</u> performed by Robert Parris, harp-
         sichord, at the Phillips Gallery, Washington, D.C.
         on January 1, 1962. "Mrs. Ballou's Rondino is a
         sophisticated study that swings from a naivete, that
         sounds in open, light dialogue, to a brilliant pow-
         erful central idea. It too found a welcome with its
         hearers." <u>See</u>: W71a

B113.   _____.   "Songs for Guitar at Gallery by 3 Popular Ar-
         tists Hailed." <u>Washington Post</u>, February 20, 1961,
         p. B6.

         Review of a recital by Charles Byrd, guitar, and
         David Baker, baritone, with Esther Ballou, piano, at
         the Phillips Gallery, Washington, D.C. The reviewer
         thought Ballou played "exemplary accompaniments," of
         works by Narvaez and Villa-Lobos.

B114.   _____.   "Symposium at American U." <u>Washington Post</u>,
         May 20, 1960, p. B9.

         Review of the May 19, 1960 performance by Gerald
         Cotts, oboe, and the American University Orchestra,
         George Steiner, conductor, of the <u>Oboe Concertino</u>.

". . . The Concertino has a lively frame for an inner portrait of grief. Its two spirited outer movements shelter an 'In Memoriam' for one of the oboe
players of the Navy Band who lost his life in the
Rio de Janeiro plane crash last February. The entire score is of distinguished material handled with
endless ingenuity. The bravura cadenza is a piece
of the utmost virtuosity in writing as its playing
must be." See: W9b

B115. _____. "Tribute to Early Training." Washington Post,
       March 27, 1969, p. C11.

       Review of the March 26, 1969 performance by Evelyn
       Swarthout of Variations, Scherzo and Fugue on a
       Theme by Lou Harrison at American University.
       "There is no little ingenuity in the variations and
       scherzo Mrs. Ballou created out of a theme by one of
       the finest and most neglected of American composers
       in music she wrote for Miss Swarthout. The fugue is
       a hand-stretching affair of mounting tensions."
       See: W80h

B116. _____. "Two Pianists Play Varied Program." Washing-
       ton Post, December 22, 1953.

       Review of Sonata for Two Pianos performed on Decem-
       ber 21, 1953 by Harry McClure and Esther Ballou at
       the Phillips Gallery, Washington, D.C. "Here the
       manner is that of Hindemith in the piling up of re-
       sounding chords in two of the movements, but the
       writing is alive and the invention does not flag.
       Composer Ballou, who knows so well the resources of
       her instrument, also knows, but does not need to
       imitate her predecessors." See: W73a

B117. "In Memoriam." Music Clubs Magazine 52/5 (Summer
       1973): 55.

       One-column notice of Ballou's death.

B118. "The Instrumental Field." Pan Pipes of Sigma Alpha
       Iota 62/1 (November 1969): 11, 18.

       Cites the recording of Prelude and Allegro on Compo-
       sers Recordings, Inc. 115. Includes a photograph of
       Ballou. See: D1

B119. Keats, Sheila, ed. "What's New." Bulletin. American
       Composers Alliance 11/2-4 (1963): 18

       Discusses the premiere of Capriccio for Violin and
       Piano at the White House. See: W19a

B120. Kriegsman, Alan M. "Anniversary Honored with Skill:
       Am. U. Completes Tribute to Genius of Debussy."
       Washington Post, March 26, 1968, p. B6.

       Review of the March 24, 1968 performance by Esther
       Ballou, piano, and Evelyn Swarthout, piano, of
       Debussy's Six Epigraphes Antiques and the American
       University Singers, Vito Mason, conductor, with
       Ballou accompanying of Debussy's La Damoiselle Elue.

B121. _____. "The Song of the Dove." Washington Post, Sep-
       tember 28, 1970, p. C6.

       Review of the "peace concert" on September 27, 1970
       in which a Ballou work was performed. No mention is
       made of the title of the work (Hear Us!). See:
       W85d, B99

B122. Krummel, D.W., Jean Geil, Doris J. Dyen, and Deane L.
       Root. Resources of American Music History: A
       Directory of Source Materials from Colonial Times to
       World War II (Urbana: University of Illinois Press,
       1981): 63.

       Describes briefly the materials in the Esther Ballou
       Memorial Collection at American University.

B123. Kyle, Marguerite K. "The Composer Amerallegro." Pan
       Pipes of Sigma Alpha Iota 55/2 (January 1963): 39.

       Cites premieres, performances, and other news re-
       garding Ballou.

B124. _____. "The Composer Amerallegro." Pan Pipes of Sig-
       ma Alpha Iota 57/2 (January 1965): 43, 46.

       Cites premieres, performances and other news regard-
       ing Ballou. Includes a photograph of Ballou.

B125. _____. "The Composer Amerallegro." Pan Pipes of Sig-
       ma Alpha Iota 60/2 (January 1968): 56, 59.

       Cites premieres and performances for 1967 and publi-
       cations and other news regarding Ballou. Includes a
       photograph of Ballou.

B126. _____. "The Composer Amerallegro." Pan Pipes of Sig-
       ma Alpha Iota 63/2 (January 1971): 48-49.

       Cites premieres, performances, publications, and
       other news regarding Esther Ballou. Includes a pho-
       tograph of Ballou.

B127. _____. "The Composer Amerallegro." <u>Pan Pipes of Sigma Alpha Iota</u> 65/2 (January 1973): 40.

Cites a performance of <u>Variations, Scherzo and Fugue on a Theme by Lou Harrison</u> performed by Evelyn Swarthout at the Kennedy Center. Mentions Ballou visiting England. <u>See</u>: W80k

B128. Learmont, John. "First Concerts: Beguine." <u>My Program Notes</u> (National Symphony Orchestra), October 9-10, 1962, p. [5].

Brief program notes for <u>Beguine</u> for the performance by the National Symphony on October 9-10, 1962 in Washington, D.C. "Esther Ballou composed the 'Beguine' after traveling to Santo Domingo in 1950. It is based on the Latin American beguine rhythm which blended the syncopation of African and Caribbean music . . . . In this piece the first melody is introduced and played several times before the second theme appears. The second theme, actually a free inversion of the main theme, is developed in the wind section. The composition closes with a combination of the two themes and the last appearance of the main theme is in the string section. Throughout the composition the Latin rhythm is dominant and emphasized by the use of exciting tambourines." <u>See</u>: W2a, W2b

B129. Leavitt, Donald L. "Spanish Works Please Throng." <u>Washington Evening Star</u>, February 20, 1961, p. A18.

Review of a recital by Charles Byrd, guitar, David Baker, baritone, and Esther Ballou, piano, on February 19, 1961 at the Phillips Gallery. "Mrs. Ballou's considerable talents were not taxed much yesterday but, as always, her accompaniments were models of assured and assuring support." Works by Milan, Narvaez, and Villa-Lobos were performed.

B130. Lowens, Irving. "Fine Recital Ends the Piano Series." <u>Washington Evening Star</u>, May 1, 1972, p. A12.

Review of the April 30, 1972 performance by Evelyn Swarthout of <u>Variations, Scherzo and Fugue</u> at the Kennedy Center for the Performing Arts. "The only other piece which communicated its meaning in a tone louder than a well-modulated, cultured mezzo-forte was Esther Williamson Ballou's 'Variations, Scherzo and Fugue on a Theme by Lou Harrison,' written especially for Miss Swarthout by the gifted Washington composer." <u>See</u>: W80k

B131.   _____.   "Kindler Recital One of Note Despite Competing
Sounds."   Washington Evening Star, June 13, 1966, p.
B11.

Review of the world premiere on June 12, 1966 of 5-
4-3 performed by Rilla Mervine, mezzo-contralto,
Richard Parnas, viola, and Sylvia Meyer, harp, at
the Textile Museum, Washington, D.C. Lowens regards
the work as "a sensitive setting of poetry by E.E.
Cummings." See: W26a

B132.   _____.   "Music: National Council Lists New Programs."
Washington Sunday Star, June 12, 1966, p. B4.

Notice of a performance of 5-4-3 to be premiered on
the evening of June 12, 1966 at the Textile Museum,
Washington, D.C. Includes a photograph of Ballou.
See: W26a

B133.   _____.   "News from Here." Washington Sunday Star,
September 1, 1963, p. B10.

Notes that Elaine Skorodin, a finalist in the Nation
Federation of Music Clubs 1963 Young Artist Audi-
tions, will be performing Ballou's Capriccio at the
White House. Includes a photograph of Ballou. See:
W19a

B134.   _____.   "Pro Arte Trio Excels in Varied Program."
Washington Evening Star, October 13, 1958, p. A17.

Review of the October 12, 1958 performance by the
Pro Arte Trio of the Trio for Violin, Violoncello,
and Piano at the Corcoran Gallery of Art, Washington, D.C. "An interesting novelty in the program
presented yesterday afternoon by the Messrs.
Engberg, Portnoy and Akers at the Corcoran Gallery
was a piano trio by Esther Williamson Ballou, a
local composer of considerable gifts. Mrs. Ballou's
music is a far cry from that of the typical 'lady
composer'. . . . The trio demonstrates a musical
intelligence of considerable imagination." See:
W41d

B135.   _____.   "Two Works by District Composers Presented."
Washington Evening Star, March 20, 1956, p. A8.

Review of the premiere of the Trio for Violin,
Violoncello, and Piano on March 19, 1956 at the
Phillips Gallery, Washington, D.C., and performed by
James Barber, violin, John Engberg, violoncello, and
Esther Ballou, piano. "Mrs. Ballou's ambitious trio
does have a certain closet vitality, but it does not

seem to have anything particularly important to
say." See: W41a

B136.   . "Violinist Treger Delight to Hear." Washington Evening Star, May 11, 1959, p. B7.

Review of a recital by Charles Treger, violin, and
Esther Ballou, piano, on May 10, 1959 at the
Corcoran Gallery of Art, Washington, D.C. "His
partner at the keyboard was Esther Ballou, who is
perhaps somewhat better known locally as a composer
than as a performer. Mrs. Ballou is an excellent
pianist indeed, and together with Mr. Treger,
treated those fortunate enough to be on hand to one
of the most notable concerts of the season." Works
by Mozart, Brahms, and Prokofiev were performed.

B137.   . "Young Artists Heard at White House." Washington Evening Star, September 7, 1963, p. A12.

Review of the September 6, 1963 premiere of
Capriccio performed by Elaine Skorodin, violin, and
Stephen Prussing, piano, at the White House. "A
significant musical 'first' took place yesterday
afternoon at the White House when a 10-minute work
by an American composer received its world premiere
in the East Room. The person so signally honored
was Esther Williamson Ballou, surely one of the most
gifted women writing music today, and a highly imaginative and skillful composer.
The piece is in Mrs. Ballou's most felicitous
vein--strong, spare and boldly contemporary. The
Capriccio is not intended to be a display piece for
a virtuoso fiddler--both artists are asked for considerable technical prowess, but fireworks are always subordinated to the music they are making.
Mrs. Ballou evidently uses the word 'capriccio' as
roughly synonymous with 'fantasia,' since the work
is serious, indeed solemn, rather than light in
mood." See: W19a

B138. Luening, Otto. The Odyssey of an American Composer:
The Autobiography of Otto Luening (New York: Charles
Scribner's Sons, 1980): 398.

Discusses the modern dance program at Bennington
College during the 1930s and mentions that Ballou
"wrote much music for the younger dancers."

B139. McCorkle, Donald M. "Benefit Concert Draws Crowd."
Washington Evening Star, March 22, 1965, p. B13.

Review of the March 21, 1965 performance at the Unitarian Church in Arlington, Virginia of four works

by Ballou: In Memoriam, performed by Beth Sears,
oboe, and members of the National Gallery Orchestra;
Early American Portrait, performed by Katherine
Hansel and members of the orchestra; Concerto for
Solo Guitar and Chamber Orchestra, performed by
Robert Luse, guitar, and members of the orchestra;
and Prelude and Allegro for String Orchestra and
Piano, performed by Esther Ballou, piano, and members of the orchestra. The conductor was Richard
Bales. "What was lacking most was a program of
quality. Esther Ballou is an eclectic composer who
obviously writes intuitively, and in variety of
styles ranging from Debussy to Piston. It is therefore difficult to pin down any particular elements
of style which are her hallmark, except perhaps her
obvious inclination to be rhapsodic, episodic, and
formally amorphous. Her melodic and harmonic textures seem to be an alternation of spare melodic
snippets and block chords.
The strongest work in the program was the opener,
the brief and elegiac In Memoriam, which makes its
mark with a fine oboe solo over low muted string
accompaniment. The Five Songs (Early American Portrait) generally lack vitality and warmth, and have
a paucity of melodic, harmonic, and rhythmic interest. They simply do not reveal enough textual con-
viction. Miss Hansel did wonders with the ungrate-
ful vocal lines, and Mrs. Ballou was admirable at
the piano.
The Guitar Concerto was one long rhapsody in which
the woodwinds and trumpet had some fairly lovely
solo work, while the strings underscored them with
parallelisms. Except for the few cadenzas, especially toward the end, the guitar could have gone
completely unnoticed, for his part was of no conse-
quence. Mrs. Ballou joined the orchestra in her
Prelude and Allegro, which combines a fantasia and
contrapuntal fast movement. The work reminds very
strongly of Walter Piston's earlier similar piece."
See: W9c, W8a, W7b, W13e, respectively. See also:
C28

B140. Margrave, Wendell. "Bales Orchestra Unusually Good."
Washington Evening Star, April 4, 1960, p. B5.

Review of In Memoriam performed by Beth Sears, oboe,
and the National Gallery Orchestra, Richard Bales,
conductor, at the National Gallery of Art, Washington, D.C. on April 3, 1960. Ballou's work ". . .
is a genuine and moving tribute to the memory of
chief musician Walter Penland, first oboist of the
Navy Band, who was one of the fine musicians killed
in the recent tragic plane crash." See: W9a

B141.   _____. "Ballou Sonata is Heard Here." Washington
         Evening Star, November 3, 1958, p. B9.

         Review of the November 2, 1958 performance by Helen
         McGraw of the Sonata for Piano at the Phillips
         Gallery. "This is a work, electric in style, in
         three movements, the first of which is a rhapsodic
         treatment of a motto theme, reminiscent a bit of
         Liszt. The second movement is for me the best of
         the three. It has long lines, sensitive handling of
         sonorities, and a certain wonderful plasticity of
         structure. The last movement, a chorale with varia-
         tions, has a definite development toward a climax,
         but appears to be more conventional in idea and in
         treatment." See: W72g

B142.   _____. "Capital Wind Quintet Shows Good Control."
         Washington Evening Star, May 19, 1966, p. C21.

         Review of a recital by the National Capital Wind
         Quintet, Mark Thomas, flute, Earnest Harrison, oboe,
         Sidney Forrest, clarinet, Jackson Bryce, bassoon,
         James London, horn, with Esther Ballou, guest
         pianist, on May 18, 1966 at American University.
         "Esther Ballou played all these piano parts deftly,
         musically and with an exquisite sense of ensemble."
         Margrave considered Ballou ". . . a gifted and
         sensitive pianist." Works by Beethoven, Roussel,
         and Verne Reynolds were performed.

B143.   _____. "Local Composers' Works in Debut." Washington
         Evening Star, May 4, 1960, p. C28.

         Review of the May 3, 1960 performance by Evelyn
         Swarthout of the Variations, Scherzo and Fugue on a
         Theme by Lou Harrison at the Corcoran Gallery of
         Art. "There followed a stunning performance by
         Evelyn Swarthout of Ester [sic] Williamson Ballou's
         second piano sonata, further described as varia-
         tions, scherzo and fuge [sic] on a theme by Lou
         Harrison. The variations began quietly with echoes
         of Couperin; the scherzo was brilliant, and I
         thought the best writing in the sonata; the fugue,
         although pianistic and reaching an excellent climax,
         stopped short of full development of the possibili-
         ties of the subject, and was, besides, strangely
         broken by several full stops." See: W80b

B144.   _____. "Works of District Composers Heard at Phillips
         Gallery." Washington Evening Star, March 8, 1955,
         p. B9.

         Review of the March 7, 1955 performance by Esther
         Ballou of her Sonata for Piano. "Esther Williamson

Ballou presented her own sonata, in three movements, for the piano. The statement of the first movement is bold, and the rhythm live and meaningful. The slow second movement extends the long arch of its melody without interruption into the chorale, which forms the theme of the last movement.

Structurally, I found only one weakness: It seemed to me that the chorale variations were foreshortened; that there was room in the theme for broader treatment. The audience liked this one." _See_: W72a, B41

B145. Mark, Michael. "Collections." _American Record Guide_ 46/5 (July 1983): 71-72.

Review of Ballou's _Sonata for Two Pianos_ (1949) recorded on Composers Recordings, Inc. 472. "The Ballou opus has in its two movements some nice examples of contrasting rhythm, lyrical moments of repose, and an attention-getting long crescendo. . . . That both performers can make what are often not the easiest ideas to digest sound forth with such clarity, and suggest a real conversation between two voices that just happen to be pianos, bespeaks a duo-piano team of real service to twentieth-century music." _See_: D2

B146. Maves, David W. "Origin of a Series: Piccolo Spoleto's Minority Artists' Project," in _The Musical Women: An International Perspective_, ed. by Judith Lang Zaimont (Westport, Conn.: Greenwood Press, 1984): 78.

Includes a concert program for May 27, 1981 at the Albert Simons Center for the Arts, College of South Carolina, Charleston, S.C. On the program was Ballou's _Street Scenes_. _See_: W98c

B147. Miller, P.L. "Recorded Music." _Library Journal_ 83/5 (1 March 1958): 747.

Cites the recording of _Prelude and Allegro_ on Composers Recordings, Inc. 115. _See_: D1

B148. Minnesota Educational Radio, Inc. _Preview_ 6/6 (June 1972): n.p.

Includes a photograph of Ballou with four additional women members of the National Federation of Music Clubs, February 13, 1970. Ballou's _Prelude and Allegro_ was broadcast over Minnesota Educational Radio on June 5, 1972, as part of a series "American Women Composers." _See_: W13

B149. Mintz, Donald. "Recital Offered by Mrs. Ballou."
       <u>Washington Evening Star</u>, May 8, 1961, p. B5.

       Review of a recital by Esther Ballou presented on
       May 7, 1961 at the Phillips Gallery, Washington,
       D.C. The critic did not enjoy this one. "If, with
       the exception of the first group [pieces by Bach and
       Scarlatti], Esther Williamson Ballou's program. . .
       had been chosen for her by a second person, one
       would say that it appeared maliciously designed to
       show her in the worst possible light." Works by
       Chopin, Schumann, and Ellis Kohs were also
       performed.

B150. _____. "Robert Parris Heard in Stunning Recital."
       <u>Washington Evening Star</u>, January 2, 1962, p. B11.

       Review of a performance by Robert Parris, harpsi-
       chord, on January 1, 1962 of <u>Rondino</u> at the Phillips
       Gallery, Washington, D.C. "The brief piece is un-
       pretentious and nice." <u>See</u>: W71a

B151. Montgomery, Merle. "We're on the Air! Its Time to
       Tune in!" <u>Music Clubs Magazine</u> 51/5 (Summer 1972):
       5, 12-14.

       Works by Ballou are broadcast over a considerable
       number of radio stations as part of American Women
       Composers, a division of the National Federation of
       Music Clubs. <u>Prelude and Allegro</u> is mentioned spe-
       cifically. <u>See</u>: W13

B152. Morrow, Grace. "Many Women Composers Hold Academic
       Posts." <u>Abilene Reporter-News</u>, March 25, 1976, pp.
       B1-B2.

       Ballou is mentioned briefly as holding an academic
       position.

B153. "Noted Composer." <u>American University Report</u> (March/
       April 1973): 3.

       Two-column notice of Ballou's death.

B154. Obituary. <u>Bognor Regis Post</u>, March 17, 1973.

       Two-column notice of Ballou's death. Includes
       biographical information. "Since she and her
       husband, Mr. Harold Ballou, moved to Felpham last
       August, they had made many friends in the area."

B155. Oja, Carol J. <u>American Music Recordings: A Discog-
       raphy of 20th-Century U.S. Composers</u> (Brooklyn,

N.Y.: Institute for Studies in American Music,
1982): 9.

Cites Composers Recordings, Inc. 115. See: D1

B156. Oliveros, Pauline. "And Don't Call Them 'Lady' Compo-
       sers." New York Times, September 13, 1970, pp. D23,
       D30.

       Esther Ballou is cited among a number of women
       composers. Reprinted in Pauline Oliveros' Software
       for People: Collected Writings 1963-80 (Baltimore:
       Smith Publications, 1984): 47-51.

B157. "Orchestra Performs." American University Eagle, May
       18, 1960, p. 8.

       Cites a symposium to take place at American
       University on May 19, 1960 in which Ballou's Oboe
       Concertino will be performed by Gerald Cotts, oboe,
       with the American University Orchestra, George
       Steiner, conducting. "The purpose of the symposium
       is to give a hearing to compositions which have not
       yet received performances." Based on this state-
       ment, it is likely the work was actually In Memoriam
       which was previously the second movement of the
       Oboe Concertino. However, In Memorian was first
       performed on April 3, 1960. See: W9b

B158. P., F.D. "Bennington Composers." New York Herald
       Tribune, March 2, 1953, p. 15.

       Review of the March 1, 1953 New York premiere of
       Fantasia Brevis I and II. ". . . Miss Williamson's
       fantasias were melodically pleasing and effectively
       scored." See: W24b; B38

B159. Parris, Robert. "At American University: Variety
       Highlights Chamber Concert in Contemporary Music
       Symposium." Washington Post, May 26, 1961, p. D12.

       Review of the May 25, 1961 performance at American
       University of Will Gay Bottje's Trumpet and Piano
       Sonata by George Foss, trumpet, and Esther Ballou,
       piano, and Linda Babits' Five by Edwin Thayer, horn,
       and Esther Ballou, piano.

B160. _____. "A Composer Reports from Washington." Bulle-
       tin. American Composers Alliance 7/3 (1958): 8.

       "The appearance of Esther Williamson Ballou in Wash-
       ington was a happy occurrence all the way around.
       She stimulated many people, not only as a composer
       but also as performer and teacher, and an increase

in this city's professional standards has without
doubt resulted from her presence on the musical
scene here."

B161.   _____. "Orchestra Returns to National Gallery."
         Washington Post, April 4, 1960, p. A23.

         Review of the April 3, 1960 performance by Beth
         Sears, oboe, and the National Gallery Orchestra,
         Richard Bales conductor, of In Memoriam at the
         National Gallery of Art, Washington, D.C. "Mrs.
         Ballou, who is one of Washington's most talented
         composers and pianists, and whose new piano sonata
         will be heard here in a few weeks, has written a
         moving response to the air tragedy in Rio de Janeiro
         a few weeks ago. It is a well-constructed, short
         piece which, unlike so much new music, sounds good.
         Conductors and oboists looking for a fairly short
         work should find this worth their time and trouble
         to investigate." See: W9a

B162.   Pavlakis, Christopher. American Music Handbook (New
         York: Macmillan, 1974): 320.

         A one-paragraph entry on Ballou; cites publishers.

B163.   "People." Symphony News 24/3 (June 1973): 23.

         "Esther Williamson Ballou, noted composer and re-
         spected teacher of piano, died March 12, 1973 in
         London, England." Includes brief biographical in-
         formation.

B164.   "Personalities." Washington Post, June 17, 1971, p.
         C7.

         News regarding a White House reception on June 16,
         1971 "for about 40 members of Sigma Alpha Iota, an
         international professional music fraternity.
         Katherine Hansel, head of the voice department of
         Catholic University, sang, accompanied by Esther
         Ballou, composer and professor at American Universi-
         ty."

B165.   Phemister, William. American Piano Concertos: A Bib-
         liography (Detroit: Information Coordinators for the
         College Music Society, 1985): 15-16.

         Includes entries for the Concerto for Piano (1965)
         and Prelude and Allegro for String Orchestra and
         Piano. Quotes excerpt from a review of the concerto
         in the Washington Post, June 7, 1965. See: W5a,
         W13, B105

B166. Porter, Cecelia H. "Music Too Far From Top Notch."
       <u>Washington Post</u>, May 5, 1969, p. B8.

       Review of the May 4, 1969 performance by Ervin
       Klinkon, violoncello, of <u>Elegy for Solo Cello</u>.
       "With its unswerving melodic concentration, the
       brief Elegy paid a persuasive tribute." <u>See</u>: W81a

B167. "Premieres." <u>BMI: The Many Worlds of Music</u> (June
       1965): 9.

       Cites the premiere of Ballou's <u>Early American Por-
       trait</u> in Arlington, Virginia. Included are excerpts
       from a review by Charles Crowder in the <u>Washington
       Post</u>. <u>See</u>: W8a, B61

B168. "Premieres." <u>BMI: The Many Worlds of Music</u> (June
       1969): 22-23.

       Cites a performance of <u>Dialogues for Oboe and Guitar</u>
       at Louisiana State University on April 11, 1969.
       Includes a photograph of Ballou. <u>See</u>: W21a

B169. "Premieres." <u>BMI: The Many Worlds of Music</u> (March
       1970): 4-5.

       Cites the premiere of <u>Prism</u> performed by the Potomac
       String Trio on October 25, 1969 in Barker Hall,
       Washington, D.C. <u>See</u>: W36a

B170. Price, Theodore. "The Composer's Problems." <u>Washing-
       ton Sunday Star</u>, March 3, 1968, pp. F1-F2.

       A discussion of six Washington, D.C. composers,
       including Esther Ballou. In a discussion of whether
       or not a composer should "push" his/her music, Price
       comments, "Esther Williamson Ballou, who teachers
       theory at American University, finds creative work
       and salesmanship incompatible. 'Getting perfor-
       mances of your music in 'The Big League' is ex-
       tremely difficult. I've long since given up on
       that. Today, you should be more of a promoter and
       more talented in administrative ability. I don't
       think composers essentially have this as part of
       their natures.'"

B171. _____. "Miss Swarthout Stars in Etudes." <u>Washington
       Evening Star</u>, March 25, 1968, p. A15.

       Review of a performance by Esther Ballou on March
       24, 1968 at the Claude Debussy Commemorative Concert
       at American University, Washington, D.C. Evelyn
       Swarthout and Esther Ballou performed Debussy's <u>Six
       Epigraphes Antiques</u>. Ballou also accompanied the

American University Singers in La Damoiselle Elue.
"The ensemble, conducted by Vito E. Mason, was well
defined and owed much to the fluent accompaniment of
Esther Ballou."

B172.   "Records in Review." High Fidelity 8/2 (February
        1958): 64, 66.

        Review of the recording of Prelude and Allegro on
        Composers Recordings, Inc. 115. "Esther Ballou's
        work for piano (excellent soloist not named) and
        orchestra has implications beyond its short length."
        See: D1

B173.   Reinthaler, Joan. "AU Choral Group is in the Dol-
        drums." Washington Evening Star, April 19, 1968, p.
        D13.

        Review of the April 17, 1968 performance of Hear Us!
        by the American University Singers at the Pan Ameri-
        can Union, Washington, D.C. ". . . a sturdy work by
        Esther Ballou called 'Hear Us,' that resembled the
        Lily [sic] Boulanger psalm settings." This article
        was printed first in the late edition of the Wash-
        ington Post, April 18, 1968 under the title "Commu-
        nication Needed: AU Choral Group Resorts to Tricks."
        See: W85b

B174.   _____. "Evelyn Swarthout: A Pianist's Pianist Does
        Her Stuff." Washington Post, May 1, 1972, p. B5.

        Review of the April 30, 1972 performance by Evelyn
        Swarthout of Variations, Scherzo and Fugue on a
        Theme by Lou Harrison at the Kennedy Center for the
        Performing Arts, Washington, D.C. "Miss Ballou's
        music is reliably competent and often very fine.
        This is one of the finest of her works that I have
        heard." See: W80k

B175.   _____. "In Top Form." Washington Post, October 29,
        1973, p. B5.

        Review of a performance by Rilla Mervine, contralto,
        and Frank Conlon, piano, of 5-4-3 at the Phillips
        Gallery, Washington, D.C., on October 28, 1973.
        Performed in memory of Esther Ballou. See: W26c

B176.   _____. "Mandel Replaces Ailing Violinist." Washing-
        ton Post, January 23, 1968, p. C11.

        Review of the January 21, 1968 performance by Alan
        Mandel of Sonata for Piano (1954) at the National
        Gallery of Art, Washington, D.C. "The Ballou sonata
        is a well-crafted piece which, for all its disso-

nances and chromaticisms, maintains tenacious hold
on its essential tonality.
   The second movement carries the intervalic motifs
of the fantasy-like first movement through unfolding
contrapuntal treatment directly into the variations
of the third on the Ainsworth Psalter hymn tune,
'Who is the Man.'" See: W72k

B177.   _____. "Of Musical and Statistical Interest." Wash-
        ington Post, November 22, 1976, p. D7.

        Review of the November 21, 1976 performance by
        Katherine Hansel, soprano, of Five Songs for Soprano
        at the Phillips Gallery, Washington, D.C. "Esther
        Ballou taught at AU, was once voted one of the top
        three woman composers, and wrote all sorts of mar-
        velous music, one work on commission by the National
        Symphony. She died several years ago leaving lots
        of music that ought to be performed.
           The five songs of her 'American Frontier' on poems
        of Elizabeth Peck are unusually dramatic pieces, the
        accompaniments occasionally orchestral in effect.
           They span a wide range of mood from pain to humor
        to gentleness to cynicism, all with great skill, and
        these moods were fully realized in Hansel's perfor-
        mance." See: W90g

B178.   _____. "Phillips Concerts: For Elmira Bier." Wash-
        ington Post, June 12, 1972, p. B7.

        Review of the June 11, 1972 performance by George
        Steiner, violin, Virginia Harpham, violin, Richard
        Parnas, viola, and John Martin, violoncello, of the
        Un Morceau d'Ensemble Sur Le Nom d'Elmira at the
        Phillips Gallery, Washington, D.C. The reviewer
        considered the work "An inventive piece. . . ."
        See: W42b

B179.   Ringenwald, Richard Donald. "The Music of Esther
        Williamson Ballou: An Analytical Study." M.A.
        thesis, American University, 1960.

        "The primary problem of research with which this
        project is concerned is the collection of material
        pertaining to a comprehensive analysis of the Sonata
        for Piano by Esther Williamson Ballou." The author
        examines briefly the educational background of
        Ballou and is based upon consultation with the com-
        poser. A survey of representative compositions
        prior to Sonata for Piano is included as is a con-
        cert program for May 18, 1960 on which Ringenwald
        performed the sonata. See: W72h

B180. Roy, Klaus George. "American Grab Bag." Hi Fi and
Music Review 1/2 (March 1958): 71-72.

A commentary of the recording of Prelude and Allegro
on Composers Recordings, Inc. 115. ". . . A deeply
felt and quite communicative piece of vital structure, influenced (favorably) by many of the century's great composers." See: D1

B181. "A Salute to Women Composers." Pan Pipes of Sigma
Alpha Iota 67/2 (January 1975): 5.

Notice of the establishment of the Esther Ballou
Memorial Collection at American University.

B182. Sayn, Elena de. "Chamber Group's Playing Called
Finest in Years." Washington Evening Star, January
5, 1953, p. A14.

Review of the January 4, 1953 performance by the
Olevsky Chamber Orchestra, Paul Olevsky, conductor,
and Esther Ballou, piano, of Prelude and Allegro.
"Esther Williamson Ballou's 'Prelude and Allegro'
for strings and piano, with the composer at the
piano, was listed twice on the program and played in
the order listed. It enjoyed an unprecedented way
of being introduced. Presented in the best possible
manner the first time, the work was easily absorbed
and understood. It was vital and exciting. But
whether the practice of playing a new composition
twice on the same program should be encouraged is
debatable." See: W13b

B183. Schonberg, Harold C. "Bennington Concert Held at the
Y.M.H.A." New York Times, March 2, 1953, p. 19.

Review of the March 1, 1953 performance by Robert
Bloom, oboe, Mary E. Jones, violin, Sonya Monosoff,
violin, A. Purcell, violin, Nellis Delay, violoncello, and Lucien Laporte, violoncello, of Fantasia
Brevis I and II. "Esther Williamson was represented
by her two short Fantasias for oboe and strings, im-
pressionistic and rather watery works." See: W25a

B184. Sears, Lawrence. "Force Highlights of Duo Pianists."
Washington Evening Star, November 16, 1971, p.B6.

Review of the November 15, 1971 recital by Evelyn
Swarthout, piano, and Esther Ballou, piano, at
American University. Ballou assisted Swarthout in
the performance of Persichetti's Concerto for Piano
for four hands. "Miss Ballou proved a worthy partner, backing up her colleague with a strong and res-
onant secundo part."

B185.   _____. "Jane White Dramatic in Ravel and Ballou."
         Washington Evening Star, November 22, 1966, p. B14.

         Review of the November 21, 1966 performance by Jane
         White, soprano, and Sara Klinkon, piano, of four
         songs from Five Songs for Soprano. "A great air of
         expectation had been built for the Ballou songs.
         The first two, Wild Geese and The Loiterer, are
         among her finest creations and formed the climax of
         the recital. Although the texts are from the moun-
         tain stories of Elisabeth S. Peck's 'American Fron-
         tier,' the composer has found them material for
         large-scale concert arias." See: W90b

B186.   _____. "Rilla Mervine Recital Rich and Interesting."
         Washington Evening Star, October 18, 1966, p. A21.

         Review of the October 17, 1966 performance of 5-4-3
         by Rilla Mervine, mezzo-contralto, Richard Parnas,
         viola, and Faith Carman, harp, at the Phillips
         Gallery, Washington, D.C. "The novelty of the
         program was the second performance of '5-4-3' (five
         songs for three performers--singer, violist and
         harpist) by Esther Williamson Ballou. These were
         commissioned by the Kindler Foundation for their
         concert last summer and are set to the unusual lower
         case poetry of e e cummings. The music is much too
         upper case and virtually has a harp glissando and a
         viola tremolando for every syllable. This reading
         had Mrs. Mervine and Parnas repeating their chores
         from the premiere, with Faith Carman replacing
         Sylvia Meyer.
           I have long been an admirer of Mrs. Ballou's
         gifts, but must confess I found these pages too
         precious to sustain interest. The audience avidly
         followed the part where the harpist threaded some of
         her strings with brown paper for a muted effect (it
         sounded like rubber bands hitting brown paper), and
         the fourth movement where she drummed a rhythm on
         the wooden frame of the harp." See: W26b

B187.   _____. "Swarthout Excels in Griffes' Sonata."
         Washington Evening Star, March 27, 1969, p. A24.

         Review of the March 26, 1969 performance by Evelyn
         Swarthout of Variations, Scherzo and Fugue on a
         Theme by Lou Harrison. "Esther Williamson Ballou's
         fine Variations Scherzo and Fugue was composed in
         1959 for Miss Swarthout. It is thoroughly
         pianistic, being based on a buoyant tune by Lou
         Harrison. A whacking good fugue finishes things
         off. Miss Ballou is represented in the current
         Schwann LP catalog with a recording of her orches-
         tral Prelude and Allegro (1955). Someone should

suggest to Miss Swarthout that she commemorate this
piece on a disc." See: W80h

B188. Secrest, Meryle. "From 8 Hands to Hands by the Dozen:
'Beguine' to Bow at Youth Concert." Washington
Post, October 8, 1962, p. B4.

Four-column feature article focusing entirely on
Ballou. Includes photograph and biographical
information. Discusses the Beguine to be performed
twice by the National Symphony Orchestra on October
9-10, 1962 in Washington, D.C. See: W2b, W2c

B189. Shaffer, Eric. [About Esther Ballou] Typescript,
December 14, 1971, American University Archives.

Biography of the composer with quotes by Ballou not
found elsewhere.

B190. "Sigma Alpha Iota Composers." Pan Pipes of Sigma
Alpha Iota 52/2 (January 1960): 24.

Two-column biography of Ballou. Cites the premiere
of Sonata for Two Pianos No 2 in August 1959 at the
SAI National Convention in San Franciso. Includes a
photograph of Ballou. See: W74a

B191. Sitton, Anna J. "Poetry Set to Music." Washington
Sunday Star, June 12, 1966, p. D3.

A three-column article based on an interview with
Ballou. Discusses the work 5-4-3, and Ballou's
sentiments regarding her approach to composition.
Includes biographical information, and a photograph
of the composer. See: W26a. "'Five poems for three
musicians' explains Mrs. Ballou of the title.
'cummings had such a gift for expressing warmth and
tenderness, as well as humor. When I first read
these poems several months ago I knew I would set
them to music. It was their content, not just the
inner rhythm, that inspired me to interpret them
musically. It means blending two completely con-
trary means of expression; something like framing a
picture. I try to say, as best I can, what the poet
is saying--but in my own idiom.' Mrs. Ballou describes the music she creates as 'just half way between conservative and avant-garde.' But there her
description ends. 'Composers do too much explain-
ing. If you could say music you wouldn't have to
write it.'"

B192. Skulsky, Abraham. "Orchestra Music." Hi-fi Music at
Home 5/3 (May 1958): 28.

Review of Composers Recordings, Inc. 115. The <u>Pre-lude and Allegro</u> is considered ". . . conventional but. . . not entirely without appeal." <u>See</u>: D1

B193. Slonimsky, Nicolas. "Ballou, Esther." <u>Baker's Biographical Dictionary of Musicians</u>, 5th ed.; <u>1971 Supplement</u> (New York: G. Schirmer, 1971): 13.

B194. _____. "Ballou, Esther." <u>Baker's Biographical Dic-tionary of Musicians</u>, 7th ed. (New York: Schirmer, 1984): 139-40.

B195. Smith, Julia. <u>Directory of American Women Composers with Selected Music for Senior and Junior Clubs</u> (Chicago: National Federation of Music Clubs, 1970): 1.

Cites address of Ballou, types of music composed, and publishers.

B196. Stern, Susan. <u>Women Composers: A Handbook</u> (Metuchen, N.J.: Scarecrow Press, 1978): 38.

Brief entry on Ballou; includes six additional sec-ondary sources.

B197. Stewart-Green, Miriam. "Women Composers' Songs: An International Selective List, 1098-1980." <u>Musical Women: An International Perspective</u>, ed. by Judith Lang Zaimont (Westport, Conn.: Greenwood Press, 1984): 286, 296-97.

Cites Esther Ballou as composing significant works. Lists and describes "The Christening" and "Wild Geese" from <u>Five Songs for Soprano</u>. <u>See</u>: W90

B198. Summers, Lorine Buffington. "Three Doctoral Disserta-tion Presentations." A.Mus.D. dissertation, Univer-sity of Michigan, 1977. <u>Dissertation Abstracts In-ternational</u> 38/11 (May 1978): 6392A-93A.

On a required dissertation recital at the University of Michigan School of Music Recital Hall on August 14, 1977, Lorine Summers, with the assistance of Beth Gilbert, piano, performed <u>Five Songs for So-prano</u>. A tape recording of the recital is available at the University of Michigan School of Music Tape Archives Recording Studio. <u>See</u>: W90j

B199. Thorpe, Day. "Cellist Olefsky Shines as Usual; But Orchestra is Disappointing." <u>Washington Evening Star</u>, March 22, 1954, p. A15.

Review of a performance by Walter Penland, oboe, and
the Olefsky Chamber Orchestra, Paul Olefsky, conductor, of the <u>Oboe Concertino</u> on March 21, 1954 at the
Phillips Gallery, Washington, D.C. "Mrs Ballou's
oboe concertino displays the solo instrument effec-
tively, and in the gigue shows itself an astringent
and rhythmically engaging study." Thorpe believes
the work refers ". . . unquestionably unconsciously,
to the fourth Beethoven piano concerto--Mrs.
Ballou's piece in the opening of its slow movement,
with ominous unison strings answered by the plaintive solo instrument. . . ." <u>See</u>: W12a, B40

B200.   _____. "Four-Hand Piano Recitalists More Pleasing by
Themselves." <u>Washington Evening Star</u>, December 22,
1953, p. B8.

Review of the December 21, 1953 performance by
Esther Ballou and Harry McClure of <u>Sonata for Two</u>
<u>Pianos</u> at the Phillips Gallery, Washington, D.C.
"The Williamson sonata for two pianos, however, was
a novelty of considerable interest, especially the
pathetic slow movement and vigorous finale."
Regarding Ballou's piano playing, Thorpe thought the
performance brilliant." Works by Bach, Mozart,
Scriabin, and Robert Evett were also performed.
<u>See</u>: W73a, B39

B201.   _____. "News of Music: Premieres Scheduled." <u>Wash-</u>
<u>ington Sunday Star</u>, March 21, 1954, p. E7.

A notice which cites the first performance of the
<u>Oboe Concertino</u> to be performed later on March 21,
1954 by Walter Penland, oboe, and the Olefsky
Chamber Orchestra, Paul Olefsky, conductor, at the
Phillips Gallery, Washington, D.C. <u>See</u>: W12a

B202.   "To Promote the Arts. . ." <u>Annual Report</u>, Edward
MacDowell Association, 1954: 7.

Cites Esther Williamson as a resident fellow at the
MacDowell Colony for May 15-October 15, 1954.

B203.   Trimble, Lester. "About the Composer," record jacket
notes (New York: Composers Recordings, Inc. 115,
1950s).

One-paragraph biography on Ballou.

B204.   Vinton, John. "Duo Presents Works by 2 D.C. Composers." <u>Washington Evening Star</u>, December 20, 1966,
p. A2.

Review of a performance by Ivan Romanenko, violin,
and Joan Singer, piano, of the <u>Capriccio for Violin
and Piano</u> at the Phillips Gallery, Washington, D.C.
on December 19, 1966. The <u>Capriccio</u> "was greeted
enthusiastically last night." <u>See</u>: W19e

B205.   _____. "Gallery Orchestra Pianist Shows Elan." <u>Wash-
ington Evening Star</u>, June 7, 1965, p. B11.

Review of the June 6, 1965 premiere performance by
Charles Crowder, piano, and the National Gallery
Orchestra, Richard Bales, conductor, of the <u>Concerto
for Piano</u> (1965) at the National Gallery of Art,
Washington, D.C. Regarding the work, Vinton states,
"This seemed an awfully home-spun affair. It contained nice sound effects now and then, but they
were stiched together in a rudimentary fashion.
Quiet passages would come to a halt and the orchestra or piano would erupt into something loud. This
would go on in four-square phrases for a while and
then some other instruments would come in with a new
idea. In the second movement, Mrs. Ballou introduced a little novelty by having percussion sounds
punctuate the melodic contours, but all this seemed
incompatible with the rest of the piece, especially
with the piano writing, which throughout was a tra-
ditional assortment of arpeggios, octaves, octave
doublings on melody lines, runs up and down, and
pounding chords." <u>See</u>: W5a

B206.   _____. "Gordon Excels in Piano Recital." <u>Washington
Evening Star</u>, January 16, 1967, p. A15.

Review of the January 15, 1967 performance by
Stewart Gordon, piano, of <u>Variations, Scherzo and
Fugue on a Theme by Lou Harrison</u> at the Tawes Recital Hall, University of Maryland at College Park.
"Highly impulsive music, as most of her works are,
it has lush textures and wide, sweeping lines at the
beginning and end, contrasting with dry, fragile
textures of only one or two notes in the middle. It
is music with many sonorous pleasures. . . . The
composer was on hand to acknowledge the enthusiastic
applause." <u>See</u>: W80g

B207. "Washington Composer Honored at White House." <u>Wash-
ington Post</u>, September 7, 1963, p. E8.

Four-column unsigned review of the premiere of
<u>Capriccio for Violin and Piano</u> at the White House on
September 6, 1963. "It is an intense piece that is
filled with strong musical ideas. In the context of
Mrs. Ballou's prolific output, this one leans more
intimately to an introspective aura of sound. It is

an angry piece that cuts a sharp swath toward being
downright furious but relinquishes its culmination
in favor of more savory cadences.
 The combine of violin and piano have been adroitly
handled. Each has its say to begin, they become to-
tally immeshed in a fashion that creates rich sonorities and then, leave one another for solo bril-
liance at the end. Each instrument is pronounced to
be its own master than submits to the social nice-
ties of ensemble.
 It is a jewel from the pen of Mrs. Ballou and is
certainly a valuable addition to the violin repertory." <u>See</u>: W19a

B208. Weinschenk, Hugo. "Piano." <u>New Records</u> 51/1 (March
 1983): 13-14.

 Review of the <u>Sonata for Two Pianos</u> (1949) recorded
 on Composers Recordings, Inc. 472. No specific comments other than "all the compositions on the album
 are worthy of serious listening." <u>See</u>: D2

B209. Zaimont, Judith Lang. "Discography." <u>Musical Woman:
 An International Perspective 1983</u> (Westport, Conn.:
 Greenwood Press, 1984): 39.

 Cites both of Ballou's commercial recordings: Composers Recordings, Inc. 115 and 472. <u>See</u>: D1, D2

Correspondence

Unless otherwise noted, original letters or photocopies of letters are held in the American University Archives. "See" references, e.g., See: B139, identify citations in the "Bibliography" section.

C1. 1935, C.H. Gray, Acting President, Bennington College, to EW.

Progress report of Esther Williamson's studies at the college.

C2. 1937 (Jun 19), Robert D. Leigh, President, Bennington College, to EW.

Discusses her academic music accomplishments while a student at Bennington; passes his thanks to her for serving on the Music Committee for graduation.

C3. 1943 (Jan 3), Janet Dulles (Mrs. John Foster Dulles) to EWB.

Thanks Ballou for her attendance and contribution to a Dulles party.

C4. 1950 (Nov 17), Richard Bales, conductor, National Gallery of Art Orchestra, to EWB.

Thanks given to Ballou for her letter; mentions a trip to Santa Domingo made by Ballou.

C5. 1951 (Feb 7), Alan Carter, Composers' Conference, Middlebury College, to EWB.

Discusses the details regarding the Sixth Annual Conference at the college. Otto Luening is also men-
tioned as a member of the executive committee for
the conference.

C6. 1953 (Dec 4), Robert Miles to EWB.

Personal news; discusses his songs.

C7. 1955 (Feb 26), Richard Franko Goldman to EWB.

Appreciation to Ballou for her nice comments on his
violin sonata. Also mentions the <u>Christmas Variations</u>
written by Ballou.

C8. 1958 (May 16), William C. Fels, President, Bennington
College, to EWB.

Appreciation to Ballou for her financial pledge to the
college.

C9. 1958 (Jun 16), Ray Green, Executive Secretary, American
Music Center, to EWB.

Requests a list of Ballou's piano works for a catalog
in preparation.

C10. 1960 (Mar 14), Ethel Butler to EWB.

Butler, who is a dancer, collaborated with Ballou on
one of the latter's works. Ballou's <u>A Passing Word</u>
will be performed by Butler on April 9, "a joint
concert sponsored by the Modern Dance Council."

C11. 1962 (Apr 6), EWB to James Coover.

Discusses her interest in a collection of Ballou
scores to be added to Vassar College. This letter and
other related correspondence is in the Dickinson Music
Library of Vassar College.

C12. 1963 (May 2), Marc Blitzstein to EWB.

Agrees to have dinner with Ballou on May 11.

C13. 1964 (Feb), Fran Hollister, student, to EWB.

A letter of admiration for Ballou's teaching
methodology.

C14. 1964 (Feb 10), Randle Elliott, President, Hood College,
to EWB.

Discusses the forthcoming award of honorary doctorate
to be awarded to Ballou on June 7.

C15. 1964 (Mar 10), Maryland Music Teachers Association to
EWB.

A commission is granted to Ballou to compose a work
for piano.

C16. 1964 (Apr 7), Helen Grimes, Secretary, Friday Morning
Music Club, to EWB.

Announces the election of Ballou to the Board of the
FMMC.

C17. 1964 (Apr 24), EWB to Grace Campbell.

Mostly personal news and regards; Ballou is excited at
the prospect of playing hostess to Mark Blitzstein,
Robert Graves, and Francis Biddle at a forthcoming
dinner in May.

C18. 1964 (Apr 24), Jim Bowling to EWB.

Congratulations to Ballou on the performance of her
work.

C19. 1964 (Apr 24), Mrs. Emory C. Smith to EWB.

Expresses her pleasure upon hearing a performance of a
Ballou work. Also mentions the performance of the
Capriccio at the White House.

C20. 1964 (May 6), Theodore Seder, Curator, Edwin A. Fleisher
Music Collection, Free Library of Philadelphia, to
EWB.

Acknowledges that Ballou's Prelude and Allegro and the
Oboe Concertino have been added to the collection.

C21. 1964 (Jun), Lloyd Ultan to EWB.

Congratulations to Ballou on her honorary doctorate.

C22. 1964 (Jun 18), Richard Bales, conductor, National Gallery Orchestra, to EWB.

Mentions Ballou's Concerto for Guitar and Concerto for
Piano (1964).

C23. 1964 (Oct 19), Oliver Daniel, Broadcast Music, Inc., to
EWB.

Daniel is pleased to have Ballou represented in the BMI journal.

C24. 1964 (Oct 20), Vanett Lawler, Executive Secretary, Music Educators National Conference, to EWB.

Thanks Ballou for sending a copy of her article for "Keyboard" for the National Student Musician; copy of article is attached to letter.

C25. 1964 (Oct 30), Iva L. Guy, President, District of Columbia Federation of Music Clubs, to EWB.

Asks Ballou to serve as judge for the 1965 Jordan Music Awards audition to be held May 2, 1965.

C26. 1964 (Nov 17), Oliver Daniel, Broadcast Music, Inc., to EWB.

Letter of appreciation to EWB for forwarding a copy of National Student Musician to him.

C27. 1964 (Dec 4), Evelyn Thorne, Editor, Mills Quarterly, to EWB.

Notifies Ballou that the journal will reprint a tribute to her honoring her award of honorary doctorate.

C28. 1965 (Mar 23), EWB to Grace Campbell.

Comments on a review by Donald McCorkle in the Washington Evening Star, March 22, 1965. See: B139

C29. 1965 (May 14), David Diamond to EWB.

Thanks Ballou for her letter and mentions her forthcoming premiere of her Concerto for Piano (1964).

C30. 1965 (Oct 11), Robert E. Farlow, Vice President, W.W. Norton, to EWB.

Thanks Ballou for her comments on Richard Franko Goldman's book Harmony in Western Music.

C31. 1965 (Oct 14), Richard Franko Goldman to EWB.

Appreciation to Ballou for her comments on his book. Mentions his violin sonata, a copy of which he is sending to her.

C32. 1965 (Oct 16), Florence Howard, Friday Morning Music Club, to EWB.

Regards Ballou's resignation from the Board of the club.

C33. 1965 (Nov 15), Hermann Berlinski, Director of Music, Washington Hebrew Congregation, to EWB.

Discusses a commission and fee to Ballou for a work to be premiered May 13, 1966.

C34. 1966 (Feb 6), Emerson Meyers, President, Kindler Foundation, to EWB.

Offers a commission from the Kindler Foundation to Ballou to write a composition for voice, harp, and either flute or viola to be performed by Sylvia Meyer and others on June 12, 1966 at the Textile Museum, Washington, D.C.

C35. 1966 (Feb 23), Arleen Heggemeier, Program Chairman, Maryland State Music Teachers Association, to EWB.

Asks Ballou to present a paper at the annual workshop to be held June 21 at the Peabody Conservatory of Music Preparatory Department.

C36. 1966 (Mar 24), Emerson Meyers, President, Kindler Foundation to EWB.

Discusses the funds allotted to Ballou's commission.

C37. 1966 (Jul), Pat Rodgers to EWB.

Asks Ballou to write a piece for forthcoming recital in March 1967.

C38. 1966 (Jul), Selma Epstein to EWB.

Informs Ballou that Angelo Gatto, conductor of a string orchestra in Baltimore, has expressed interest in any works composed by Ballou for string orchestra.

C39. 1966 (Jul 25), William Bennett, Musical Director, Washington Civic Symphony, to EWB.

Bennett offers a commission to Ballou to write a wind octet or similar ensemble.

C40. 1966 (Nov 18), Aaron Copland to EWB.

Regarding a photograph of Copland.

C41. 1966 (Nov 18), Lionel Nowak, Director of Development, Bennington College, to EWB.

Mentions the prestige Ballou has brought to Bennington College.

C42. 1967 (Jan 7), David Diamond to EWB.

Comments on EWB composition and requests a copy of a tape recording of his string quartet which was performed at American University.

C43. 1967 (Mar 20), John Ciardi, Poetry Editor, Saturday Review, to EWB.

Permission granted to Ballou to set Ciardi's poem "Returning Home" to music.

C44. 1967 (May 17), Jane White to EWB.
On the performance of songs by Ballou.

C45. 1967 (Dec 11), Lionel Nowak to EWB.

Nowak's reaction to Ballou's approach to teaching history and styles of music; mentions Ballou's Capriccio.

C46. 1968 (Jan 5), Robert W. Miller, Office of the President, American University, to EWB.

Letter of appreciation to Ballou "for writing the special choral piece for the February 24 75th Anniversary Convocation."

C47. 1968 (Feb 26), Milton Babbitt to EWB.

Discusses the structure of his Composition for Four Instruments.

C48. 1968 (Feb 29), Hubert H. Humphrey to EWB.

Congratulations on Ballou's Hear Us! as performed by the American University Singers.

C49. 1968 (Sep 7), EWB to Lloyd Ultan.

Personal news regarding Ballou's trip to Nantucket.

C50. 1968 (Dec 8), Willard George to EWB.

Discusses the enjoyable time visiting with the Ballou family; mentions a choral work by Ballou.

C51. 1969 (Jan 24), EWB to Lloyd Ultan.

Personal news; mentions in some detail an electronic workshop she attended at Catholic University of America.

C52. 1969 (Jul 22), Marion M. Richter, Chairman, American
     Music Department, National Federation of Music Clubs,
     to EWB.

     Congratulations to Ballou for winning Honorable
     Mention in the NFMC-ASCAP National Awards to American
     Women Composers Program.

C53. 1969 (Aug 2), EWB to Mrs. Alfred J. Bowen.

     Biographical information submitted by Ballou on behalf
     of an award presented to her by American Women Compo-
     sers.

C54. 1970 (May 18), Edna H. Benzinger, Chairman, Young Compo-
     sers Contest, National Federation of Music Clubs, to
     EWB.

     Asks Ballou to serve as one of the judges for the 1971
     Young Composers Contest.

C55. 1971 (May 23), Donna Williams to EWB.

     Discusses her recent move to Munich, and various musi-
     cal events occuring in Europe.

C56. 1971 (Jun 2), Ruth C. Gould, National President, Sigma
     Alpha Iota, to EWB.

     Letter of "invitation to be with members of Sigma
     Alpha Iota for the Honorary Patroness initiation cere-
     monies for Mrs. Richard M. Nixon on Wednesday, June
     16, 1971, at 2:30 P.M. in the White House."

C57. 1971 (Jun 25), Patricia Nixon to EWB.

     Letter of appreciation for initiating the First Lady
     as honorary patroness of Sigma Alpha Iota and for
     Ballou's "beautiful piano playing."

C58. 1971 (Jun 26), Ruth C. Gould, National President, Sigma
     Alpha Iota, to EWB.

     Letter of appreciation for Ballou's contribution to
     the initiation service for First Lady Patricia Nixon.

C59. 1971 (Sep 24), Joan H. Joshi, Division of Study Abroad,
     Institute of International Education, to EWB.

     Regards to Ballou who "will assist in the selection of
     applicants for Fulbright-Hays and foreign-sponsored
     awards for study in music."

C60. 1971 (Nov 9), EWB to Julian DeGray.

Ballou informs DeGray of her forthcoming trip to New York on December 9 and requests a piano lesson with him. She also mentions her forthcoming piano recital with Evelyn Swarthout on November 15.

C61. 1971 (Nov 13), Julian DeGray to EWB.

Discusses Ballou's forthcoming participation in the Fulbright-Hays program on December 9 in New York, as well as casual plans while there. Also mentions her piano recital on November 15; mentions a number of music personalities.

C62. 1972 (Jan 4), Kenneth Holland, President, Institute of International Education, to EWB.

Regards and appreciation to Ballou for participation in the Fulbright-Hays program.

C63. 1972 (Feb 6), Charles Crowder to EWB.

Crowder offers Ballou a commission to compose a work in honor of Elmira Bier to be performed at the Phillips Gallery in June 1972.

C64. 1972 (Mar 12), Charles Crowder to EWB.

Details regarding performances of Ballou's compositions on June 10-11, 1972 at the Phillips Gallery, Washington, D.C.

C65. 1972 (Nov 25), EWB to Lloyd Ultan.

Personal news; mentions a new "composer in residence" idea for American University proposed by Ultan; mentions her National Youth Orchestra commission given to her for a piano concerto.

C66. 1972 (Dec 3), EWB to Lloyd Ultan.

Personal news; mentions that she wrote to Donna Williams, her former student.

C67. 1973 (Jan 7), EWB to Lloyd Ultan.

Personal news; discusses matters regarding American University and her health.

C68. 1973 (Feb 25), Elizabeth Vrenios (Kirkpatrick) to EWB.

Personal regards and news about musical events at American University.

Appendix I: Discography

This list includes all commercially-produced discs, whether or not currently available. "See" references, e.g., See: B202, identify citations in the "Bibliography" section. Private recordings of many of Ballou's works are held in the American University Archives.

D1. PRELUDE AND ALLEGRO FOR STRING ORCHESTRA AND PIANO
    (1951)

    Composers Recordings, Inc. CRI 115. [1958].
    Vienna Orchestra; F. Charles Adler, conductor.
    Pianist not cited.
    Mono; program notes, "About the Composers," by Lester
        Trimble. See: B202.
    Also includes works by Hermann Berlinski and Edwin
        Gerschefski.
    See: B22, B23, B33, B81, B118, B147, B155, B172, B180,
        B192, B209

D2. SONATA FOR TWO PIANOS (1949)

    Composers Recordings, Inc. CRI SD 472. 1982.
    Toni and Rosi Grunschlag, duo-pianists.
    Stereo; program notes, "Esther Williamson Ballou:
        Sonata for Two Pianos (1949)." See: B76.
    Also includes works by Paul Hindemith, Norman Dello
        Joio, and Darius Milhaud.
    See: B83, B86, B145, B208, B209

Appendix II: Interviews and Other Audio Sources

"See" references, e.g., <u>See</u>: W53a, identify citations in the "Works and Performances" section.

A1. 1961 (Nov 12), EWB guest appearance on educational television series (Washington, D.C.; 15 min.)

   1 audio reel tape.
   D.C. station unnamed
   Host: Mrs. Haywood
   On this children's program, Ballou discusses the art of composing by playing examples of intervals and rhythms. She also performs a number of her works, including "Rigaudon" and "Gigue" from <u>Dance Suite</u> and <u>Street Scenes</u> with soprano Jeanne Gage. <u>See</u>: W53a, W98a, respectively

A2. 1962 (Mar 28), Gordon Smith interviews EWB (Washington, D.C.; 58 min.)

   1 audio reel tape.
   Series: <u>Musicians Face the Music</u>.
   Radio station WAMU on the campus of American University.
   Discusses various aspects of Ballou's career and the compositions cited below.
   Includes performances of <u>Sonata for Piano</u> (Esther Ballou, piano), <u>Suite for Winds, In Memoriam for Oboe and String Orchestra, A Passing Word</u> (excerpt), and <u>Variations,Scherzo and Fugue on a Theme by Lou Harrison</u> (Evelyn Swarthout, piano). <u>See</u>: W72, W39, W9, W109, W80, respectively

A3. 1962 (Apr 21), Tory Baker interviews EWB (Chevy Chase, Md.; 14 min.)

    1 audio reel tape.
    Series: The Feminine Touch, no. 69.
    Voice of America broadcast.
    Ballou discusses how she composes, where her musical ideas come from and how musicians should be trained. She also explains her definition of American music and her appreciation of jazz.

A4. 1966 (Apr 20), "Music in the Atomic Age"; panel discussion (Washington, D.C.; 30 min.)

    1 audio reel tape.
    WRC-TV.
    Members of the American University Music Department faculty.
    Host: Gordon H. Smith.
    Participants: Esther Ballou, James McLain, and Lloyd Ultan.
    Series: University Colloquium.
    Discusses contemporary abstract music using Karlheinz Stockhausen as the principal example. About Stockhausen's tape music, Ballou comments, "I think his use of familiar sounds that we hear in everyday life, in this abstract way, is extremely interesting. To me it's completely foreign. I'm not able to think in this kind of idiom at all, myself." About Otto Luening, she explains, "I was around Bennington when he was experimenting in 1937. . . . He was already doing things with the flute, playing upside-down, backwards, I mean the tape can be reversed, you know."

A5. 1966 (Oct 17), Gordon Smith interviews EWB (Washington, D.C.; 11 min.)

    1 audio reel tape.
    Intermission interview.
    For broadcast over radio station WAMU.
    Discusses her work 5-4-3; includes a performance at the Phillips Gallery. See: W26b

A6. 1966 (Dec 19), Gordon Smith interviews Ivan Romanenko, violinist (Washington, D.C.; 10 min.)

    1 audio reel tape.
    Intermission interview..
    For broadcast over radio station WAMU.

Discusses Ballou's <u>Capriccio for Violin and Piano</u>; includes his performance of the work at the Phillips
Gallery. <u>See</u>: W19e

A7.   1974 (Oct 16), Julian DeGray, a tribute to EWB
(Bennington, Vt.; 10 min.)

3 audio reel tapes.
"Bennington College Presents Music by Esther
Williamson Ballou."
DeGray discusses Ballou's student days at Bennington
College during the 1930s, and her later illness.
Includes performances of <u>Trio for Violin, Violoncello,
and Piano</u>, <u>5-4-3</u>, <u>Forty Finger Beguine</u>, and <u>Adagio
for Bassoon and String Orchestra</u>. <u>See</u>: W41f, W26d,
W56b, W1a, respectively

Appendix III: Esther Williamson Ballou: A Self-Evaluation (1970)

I love music. I love people--all kinds. I love to read. I
love to laugh. I am fascinated by ideas. I have infinite
patience, IF it is deserved. I admire ambition, but do not
cherish it. I do cherish sincerity. I abhor casualness and
laziness, especially in someone who is gifted. I demand
humility toward the greatness of such as Bach. Novelty for
its own sake bores me. Hypocrisy appalls me.

I have a real gift for sensing people and their inner moti-
vations. My main target in teaching is to bolster and foster
and develop, in every way felt and known to me, the inner
needs of a student for a realization of his native potential.
Encouragement was not wisely given to me in my early life.
Perhaps this accounts for my need to give it wholeheartedly
to others.

I am stubborn and very demanding towards myself, and never
seem to be able to learn enough--well enough--but I keep
working and studying. Daily wear and tear sometime make it
difficult to be challenging, but my average is high. There
never seems to be enough time for what needs doing and this
sometimes makes me impatient with students who are not doing
their best. I am fascinated with the constant interplay
between intellect and emotion in every facet of life.
Ponderous pomposity, self-consciously structured theories and
superficial philosophizing are my special hates.

I love clarity and simplicity in the expression of truth, as
in the music of Mozart. And since music flows through me
like a current, it must be the means of communication I can
best utilize. That is why I teach it. (Esther Ballou Personal
Papers, American University Archives.)

Appendix IV: Alphabetical List
of Compositions

Numbers following each title, e.g., W102, refer to the
"Works and Performances" section of this volume.

Accompaniments for Modern Dance Technique, W102
Adagio for Bassoon and String Orchestra, W1
Allegro (In First Position) for String Quartet, W16
Art of the Fugue: Contrapunctus V [and] IX," W47
A Babe is Born, W82
Bag of Tricks, W83
The Beatitudes, W84
Beguine for Orchestra, W2
Beguine for Two Pianos, W48
Berceuse for Piano, W49
Blues, W17
Blues for Orchestra, W3
Brass Sextette with Pianoforte, W18
Bride, W89
Brown Orchids, W50
Capriccio for Violin and Piano, W19
Christmas Variations for Recorder or Oboe and Harpsichord,
  W20
Chromatic Invention, W51
Class in Music, W103
Concerto for Piano (1945), W4
Concerto for Piano (1964), W5
Concerto for Piano (1972), W6
Concerto for Solo Guitar and Chamber Orchestra, W7
Country Dance for Piano, W52
Dance Suite: "Prelude; Rigaudon; Sarabande; Galliarde;
  Courante; Bouree; Gigue," W53
Dialogues for Oboe and Guitar, W21
Discussion of 'Maan' for Oboe and Guitar, W22
Divertimento for String Quartet, W23
Early American Portrait, W8

Earth Saga, W104
Elegy for Solo Cello, W81
11 Piano Teaching Pieces, W54
Fantasia Brevis for Oboe and Strings, W24
Fantasia Brevis No. II for Oboe and String Quartet, W25
5-4-3, W26
Five Songs for Soprano, W90
For Art Nagle on His Birthday, W55
Forty Finger Beguine for Two Pianos, W56
Four Songs, W91
Four-Hand Suite, W57
Fugato, W105
Haiku, W27
Hear Us!, W85
I Will Lift Up Mine Eyes, W86
Impertinence for Clarinet and Piano, W28
Impertinence for Two Pianos, W58
Impromptu for Organ, W59
In Blues Tempo (clarinet and piano), W29
In Blues Tempo (piano, four hands), W60
In Memoriam for Oboe and String Orchestra, W9
Intermezzo for Orchestra, W10
Jazz Theme and Variations, W61
Konzertstück for Viola and Orchestra, W11
Lament for Violoncello and Piano, W30
Let-Down for Oboe or Violin and Piano, W31
Lysistrata, W106
Madchen in Uniform, W107
May the Words, W87
Merely a Beginning--Stage Fright, W108
Minutiae for Flute and Piano, W32
Music for the Theatre for Two Pianos, W62
Nocturne for String Quartet, W33
O the Sun Comes Up-Up-Up in the Opening, W88
Oboe Concertino for String Orchestra and Oboe, W12
Overture "Of Thee I Sing," W63
Passacaglia and Toccata for Organ, W64
A Passing Word, W109
Piece for Piano (untitled), W65
A Plaintive Note [and] A Cheerful Note, W34
Pocohantas Goes to London: A Musical Comedy, W110
Pop Goes the Weasel, W111
Portrait I, W66
Prelude, W112
Prelude and Allegro for String Orchestra and Piano, W13
Prelude and Gigue for Piano, W67
Prelude Number 1, 2, and 3 for Piano, W69
Prelude I for Piano, W70
Preludes for Piano, W68
Pride, Envy, Sloth, Lust, Anger, W35
Prism for String Trio, W36
Quest for the Dance, W113
Romanza or L'Histoire d'un Romance, W37
Rondino for Harpsichord, W71

Rumba on Riverside Drive, W92
The Sea in Maine: The Presence of the Sea, W93
The Shepherd, W94
Sonata for Piano, W72
Sonata for Two Pianos, W73
Sonata for Two Pianos No. 2, W74
Sonatina, W75
Sonatina No. 2, W76
A Song (1938), W95
A Song (1949), W96
A Song (1967), W97
Street Scenes, W98
Suite for Chamber Orchestra, W14
Suite for Solo Guitar and String Orchestra, W15
Suite for Violoncello and Piano, W38
Suite for Winds, W39
A Telephone Number, W77
Theme and Variations on Shenandoah Alma Mater, W40
Time, W99
Tree of Sins, W114
Trial Run, W115
Trio for Violin, Violoncello, and Piano, W41
Triumphant Figure, W78
Un Morceau d'Ensemble sur le nom d'Elmira for String Quartet,
    W42
Up into the Silence, W100
Variations for Gail, W79
Variations, Scherzo and Fugue on a Theme by Lou Harrison, W80
Violin and Pianoforte Sonata, W43
Violin Sonatina, W44
War Lyrics, W116
What if a Much of a Which of a Wind, W45
Whip-Poor-Will, W101
Wind Quintette, W46

Appendix V: Chronological List of Compositions

Numbers following each title, e.g., W17, refer to the "Works and Performances" section of this volume.

1930s   Blues, W17
Lysistrata, W106
Madchen in Uniform, W107
Overture "Of Thee I Sing," W63

1933-37   Accompaniments for Modern Dance Technique, W102

1936   Impertinence for Clarinet and Piano, W28
Impertinence for Two Pianos, W58
Jazz Theme and Variations, W61

1937   Country Dance for Piano, W52
Dance Suite: "Rigaudon, Galliarde, Courante, Bouree,
   Gigue," W53
Four Songs, W91
In Blues Tempo (clarinet and piano), W29
In Blues Tempo (piano, four hands), W60
Let-Down for Oboe or Violin and Piano, W31
Merely a Beginning--Stage Fright, W108
Nocturne for String Quartet, W33
Time, W99

1937-38   Violin and Pianoforte Sonata, W43

1938   Earth Saga, W104
A Song, W95

1939   Prelude Number 1, 2, and 3 for Piano, W69
Suite for Chamber Orchestra, W14

1940s   Pocohantas Goes to London: A Musical Comedy, W110

        Prelude, W112
        Rumba on Riverside Drive, W92

1940   Class in Music, W103
        War Lyrics, W116

1940-41 Preludes for Piano, W68

1941   Sonatina, W75

1942   Brown Orchids, W50

1943   Allegro (In First Position) for String Quartet, W16
        Intermezzo for Orchestra, W10
        Pop Goes the Weasel, W111

1944   Blues for Orchestra, W3
        The Shepherd, W94

1945   Concerto for Piano, W4
        Lament for Violoncello and Piano, W30

1948   Prelude and Gigue for Piano, W67

1949   Sonata for Two Pianos, W73
        A Song, W96

1950s   11 Piano Teaching Pieces, W54

1950   Fantasia Brevis for Oboe and Strings, W24
        Forty Finger Beguine for Two Pianos, W56

1951   Music for the Theatre for Two Pianos, W62
        A Plaintive Note [and] A Cheerful Note, W34
        Prelude and Allegro for String Orchestra and Piano,
            W13
        Suite for Violoncello and Piano, W38

1952   Fantasia Brevis No. II for Oboe and String Quartet,
            W25

1953   Dance Suite: "Prelude," W53
        Minutiae for Flute and Piano, W32
        Oboe Concertino for String Orchestra and Oboe, W12
        Wind Quintette, W46

1954   Christmas Variations for Recorder or Oboe and
            Harpsichord, W20
        Sonata for Piano, W72

1955   Trio for Violin, Violoncello, and Piano, W41

1956   Bag of Tricks, W83
        Berceuse for Piano, W49

1957   The Beatitudes, W84
         Beguine for Two Pianos, W48
         Four-Hand Suite, W57
         Suite for Winds, W39

1958   Divertimento for String Quartet, W23
         Sonata for Two Pianos No. 2, W74

1959   A Babe is Born, W82
         Variations, Scherzo and Fugue on a Theme by Lou
            Harrison, W80
         Violin Sonatina, W44
         What if a Much of a Which of a Wind, W45

1960s   Fugato, W105
         Piece for Piano (untitled), W65
         A Telephone Number, W77
         Triumphant Figure, W78

1960   Adagio for Bassoon and String Orchestra, W1
         Beguine for Orchestra, W2
         In Memoriam for Oboe and String Orchestra, W9
         A Passing Word, W109
         Prelude I for Piano, W70
         Pride, Envy, Sloth, Lust, Anger, W35
         Quest for the Dance, W113
         Street Scenes, W98
         Tree of Sins, W114

1961   Dance Suite: "Sarabande," W53
         Rondino for Harpsichord, W71

1962   Brass Sextette with Pianoforte, W18
         Bride, W89
         Early American Portrait, W8
         Five Songs for Soprano, W90
         Passacaglia and Toccata for Organ, W64
         The Sea in Maine: The Presence of the Sea, W93
         Whip-Poor-Will, W101

1963   Art of the Fugue: "Contrapunctus V [and] IX," W47
         Capriccio for Violin and Piano, W19

1964   Concerto for Piano, W5
         Concerto for Solo Guitar and Chamber Orchestra, W7
         Sonatina No. 2, W76
         Variations for Gail, W79

1965   I Will Lift Up Mine Eyes, W86
         May the Words, W87

1966   Dialogues for Oboe and Guitar, W21
         Discussion of 'Maan' for Oboe and Guitar, W22
         5-4-3, W26

O the Sun Comes Up-Up-Up in the Opening, W88

1967   Hear Us!, W85
         A Song, W97

1968   Elegy for Solo Cello, W81
         For Art Nagle on His Birthday, W55
         Haiku, W27
         Impromptu for Organ, W59
         Portrait I, W66
         Up into the Silence, W100

1969   Konzertstück for Viola and Orchestra, W11
         Prism for String Trio, W36
         Romanza or L'Histoire d'un Romance, W37
         Trial Run, W115

1972   Concerto for Piano, W6
         Un Morceau d'Ensemble sur le nom d'Elmira for String
             Quartet, W42

no date Chromatic Invention, W51
         Suite for Solo Guitar and String Orchestra, W15
         Theme and Variations on Shenandoah Alma Mater, W40

Index

RECENT TITLES IN
BIO-BIBLIOGRAPHIES IN MUSIC
SERIES ADVISERS: DONALD L. HIXON AND ADRIENNE FRIED BLOCK

Thea Musgrave: A Bio-Bibliography
Donald L. Hixon

Aaron Copland: A Bio-Bibliography
JoAnn Skowronski

Samuel Barber: A Bio-Bibliography
Don A. Hennessee

Virgil Thomson: A Bio-Bibliography
Michael Meckna and Donald L. Hixon